The Scribner Book of Embroidery Designs

The Scribner Book of Embroidery Designs

MURIEL BAKER, EDITOR

Charles Scribner's Sons, New York

Library of Congress Cataloging in Publication Data
Main entry under title:
The Scribner book of embroidery designs.
    1. Embroidery—Patterns.   I. Baker, Muriel L.
TT771.S37   746.4′4   79-9062   ISBN 0-684-16237-7

Printed in the United States of America.

1 3 5 7 9 11 13 15 17 19 MD/C 20 18 16 14 12 10 8 6 4 2

Contents

The Scribner Book of Embroidery Designs

Introduction

Here is a book that is truly different. It contains thirty-six embroidery designs from some of the finest teachers and designers of our time. Most of them are nationally known; this is the debut of one or two. On these pages are not only their designs, but their thoughts on working them. Each is individually presented and has the imprint of the person whose work it is.

Except where unusual stitches have been employed, stitch charts have not been included. There are many fine stitch books readily available. However, text and charts show *where* stitches are used. Color suggestions have also been included.

Eleven different techniques are shown: crewel, canvas, blackwork, pulled threads on both fabric and canvas, cross-stitch, silk and metallic threads in both secular and church work, stump work, white work, hedebo on both fabric and canvas, and two designs showing a combination of techniques.

I sincerely wish to thank these nineteen artists for allowing me to share with you their exceptional talents. And my appreciation also goes to photographers John Ogden Studios, Charles Haralson, Loy Westbury, Harold Pratt, Chet Brickett, Bob Talley, Philip Bergh, Patricia Lambert, David Feisner, Helen Wilson Sherman, Lee Angle Photography Ltd., Armen Tachjian, Al LeClaire, Jan Thacher, Henry Rorden, Photo Dynamics, Don Servais, Jack Kausch, and McKenzie Dickerson for their photographic expertise. Aren't their pictures lovely?

As well, my thanks to all others—and there were many—especially Barbara Eyre for extra help and Jeanne Simpson for typing the manuscript.

I hope you will find this a book to treasure as well as to use and enjoy.

Muriel Baker
March 1979

Little Town at Dusk

BETTY BOHANNON

See Color Plate 1.

Photo by John Ogden Studios.

Overall Size: 10" x 12".

MATERIALS

18-mesh canvas—13" x 15"
20-40-mesh canvas—8" x 8", 5" x 5", and 5" x 5"
6-strand embroidery floss
Crewel or Persian wool

DIRECTIONS

In the following Directions, an asterisked (*) instruction indicates that you should turn the canvas by a one-quarter turn and stitch normally—for example, reverse tent direction.

Bakery

1*: Alternating rows diagonal tent stitch, one row dark blue floss, one row white crewel

1A*: Diagonal Scotch stitch, light blue floss

1B: Leave void eleven strands of bare canvas

Florist
2: Mosaic stitch, alternating shades light and medium light gold floss
2A: Leave void fourteen strands of bare canvas
2B: Parisian stitch, alternating color, medium and dark gold floss (nine strands)
2C: Slanting Gobelin stitch, medium light gold floss

Pink House
3: Mosaic stitch, medium light coral floss
3A: Diagonal mosaic stitch (Florence stitch), medium dark coral
3B: Tent stitch, dark coral floss
3C: Tent stitch, medium light coral floss
3D: Slanted Gobelin stitch, medium coral floss

Gold House
4*: Double tent stitch, alternating rows medium and dark gold floss
4A: Diagonal tent stitch, light gold floss
4B: Diagonal tent stitch, alternating rows light and dark gold floss

Castle
5: Space windows evenly, three vertical continental stitches, charcoal floss
5A*: Twin bricking stitch, two strands light gray crewel
5B: Space three windows in turret, cashmere charcoal floss
5C*: Twin bricking stitch, light gray and medium gray, one strand each, in needle
5D*: Twin bricking stitch, light gray and medium gray crewel

Church
6*: Single bricking stitch, light gray crewel (two strands)
6A*: Single bricking stitch, gray shades light and dark, one strand each, in needle, crewel
6B: Diagonal mosaic stitch, charcoal floss
6C: Diagonal tent stitch, charcoal floss

Rectory
7*: Diagonal tent stitch, medium light coral floss
7A*: Diagonal tent stitch, medium coral floss

Mountains
8: Encroaching Gobelin stitch, medium blue-green crewel
9: Encroaching Gobelin stitch, light blue-green crewel

Garden
10: Smyrna cross-stitch, dark gold crewel; French knots in bright floss for flowers

Trees
11: Diagonal tent stitch, crewel yarn, light blue-green, dark blue-green outline crewel; medium gold tent stitch for trunk, crewel

Bulkhead
12: Old Florentine stitch, medium brown crewel

Bridge
13: Old Florentine stitch, medium gold floss (nine strands); handrail, brick stitch, medium light gold floss (nine strands)

Water
14: Kalem stitch over 2″ x 2″ canvas threads, light and dark aqua-blue floss

Path
15*: Single bricking stitch, light gold crewel

Grass
16: Using yarn, with tent stitch, use medium green crewel for grass and for base of picture (the near bank)

Sky
17: Light blue crewel, use double encroaching Gobelin stitch (Soumac); white crewel for clouds

DIRECTIONS FOR CUTTING CANVAS (after completing 18-mesh picture)

Bakery
Eleven bare canvas threads both directions, start cutting at the first bare thread in the window. In the *center* of alternate vertical threads, cut one, leave one uncut—until five panes are cut.
With polyester thread and regular sewing needle, tie back the cut ends in lasso fashion on back of work.

Florist
Same as above: Cut the first two vertical threads in the center of the thread, leave one uncut, and continue as in the bakery—having five panes when complete. Cut two horizontal threads, leave one uncut as above.

Inside of florist and bakery windows: one 8″ x 8″ piece of 20-40 mesh.

Bakery
Birthday cake: Medium coral floss and white floss
Rolls and donuts: Light gold, two strands floss
Drapes (as drawn): Dark blue, two strands floss
Background: Double tent stitch, medium blue, two strands floss

Bakery

Florist

Hanging baskets and plants: Flowers, French knots varied colors of floss; leaves, light green floss

Drapes (as drawn): Medium gold floss, three strands

Background: Double tent stitch, light gold floss, two strands

Florist

When complete, sew in place securely behind the open store windows.
Using a #24 or #26 needle, letter signs on 5-inch 20-40 mesh, ravel canvas, baste signs on securely, and work canvas threads through 18-mesh canvas to back of piece and weave in.

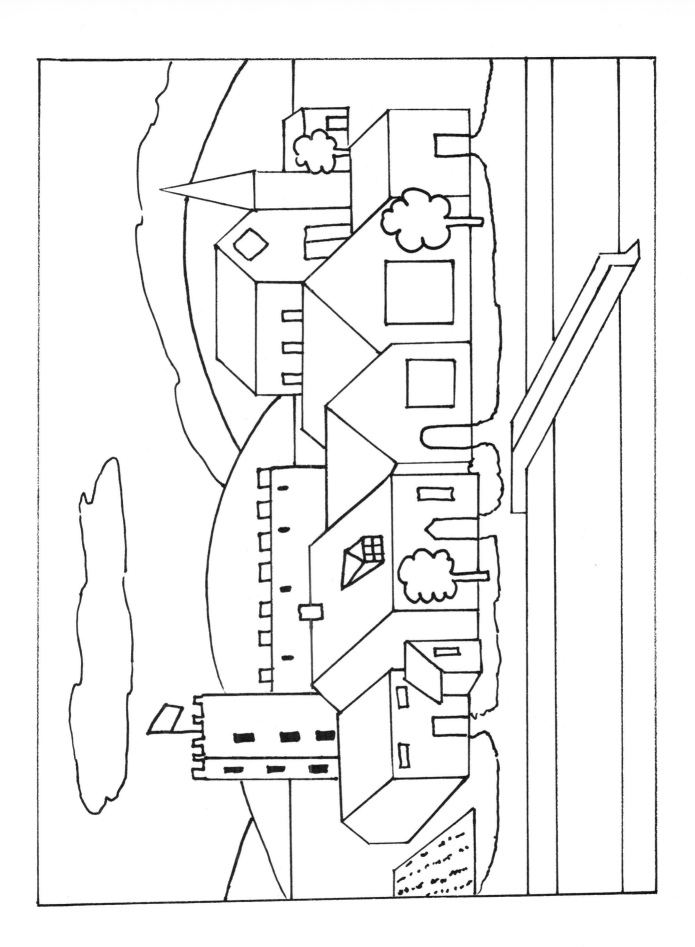

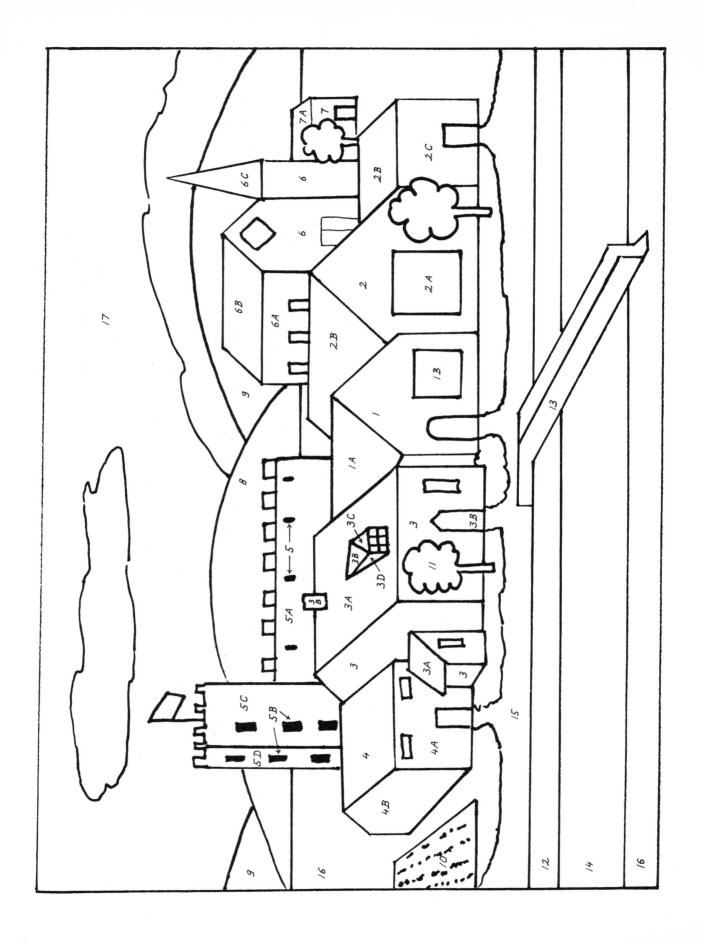

Photo by Charles W. Haralson.

Checkerboard

MARION SCOULAR

Overall Size: 15½" x 15½".

MATERIALS

22-inch square of white Davos
Six 25-yard skeins of D.M.C. Coton à Broder #12
#22 chenille needle

Counted threadwork is normally worked with a tapestry needle. It is much easier to make work even if a chenille needle is used when working with Coton à Broder on Davos.

DIRECTIONS

Baste two lines to mark the centers of the fabric each way. Then baste four lines on each side of these lines, counting thirty-two threads, thus creating a total of sixty-four squares. Attach the material to a 27-inch rotating frame with 15-inch side arms. Work the patterns in alternating squares as shown.

All patterns are symmetrical and counted in pairs of threads, with the exception of the following numbers: 5, 12, 15, 28. These will involve compensation stitches over one fabric thread.

Pattern number 26 should be worked by counting from the center of the square.

Outline each square in double running—over two threads, under two threads. The border pattern can also be worked in double running.

If you make a mistake, the unpicked stitches will leave black dots on the fabric that are almost impossible to remove, so stitch carefully. It is a good idea to place your waste knot on one of the borders so that the dot left when you cut it off will be covered by the outline.

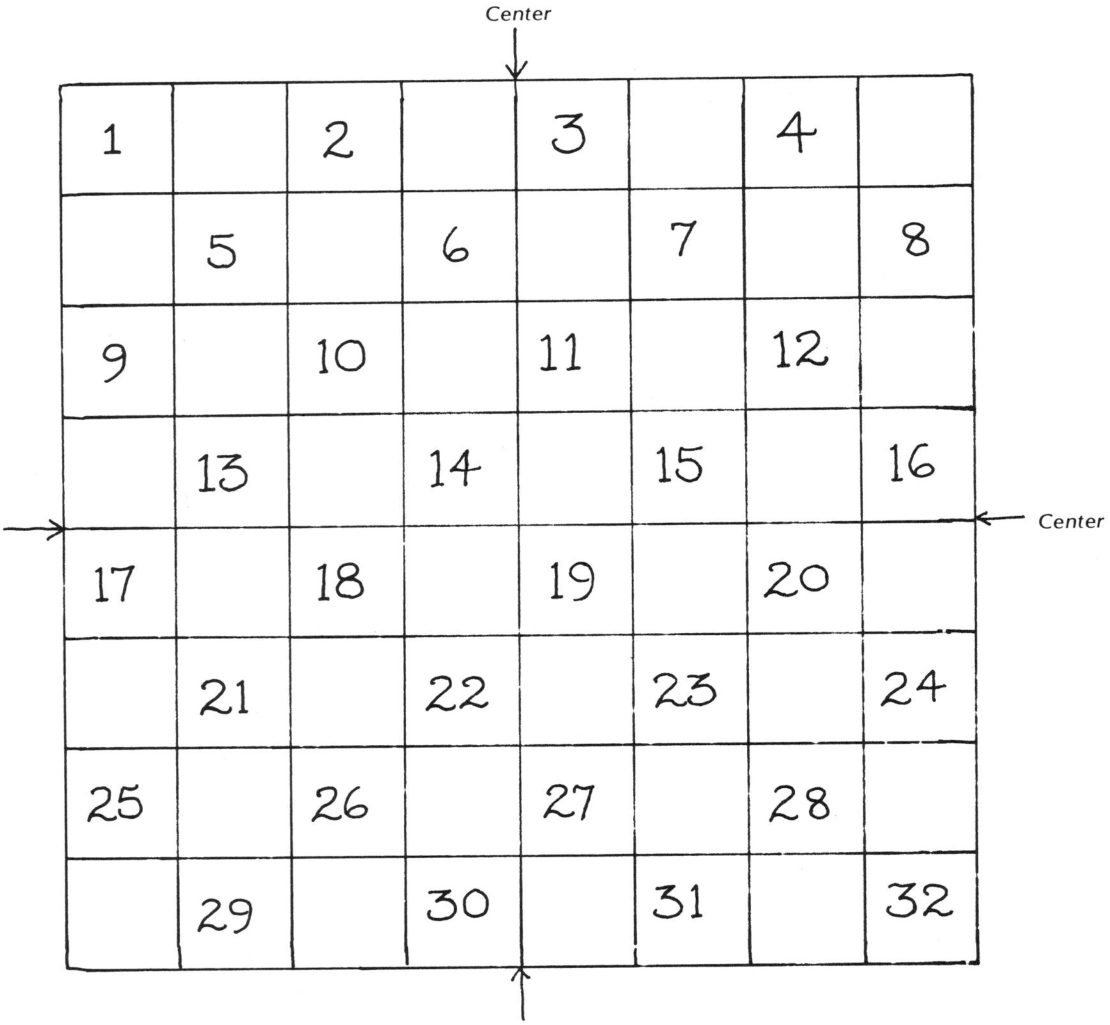

Center

1	2	3	4
5	6	7	8
9	10	11	12
13	14	15	16
17	18	19	20
21	22	23	24
25	26	27	28
29	30	31	32

Center

Placement of Stitches for Checkerboard

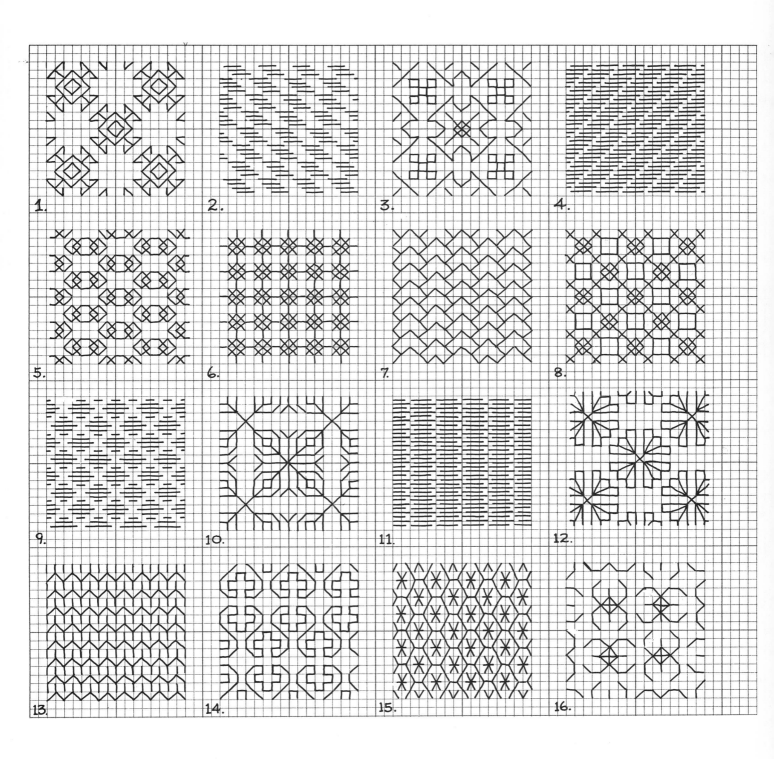

One square of the graph paper = two intersections of the fabric.

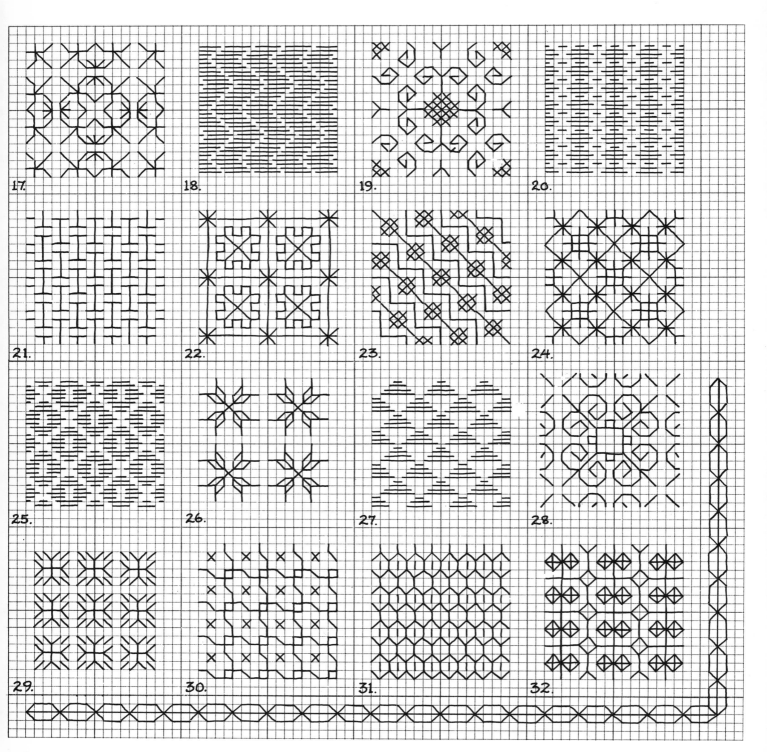

One square of the graph paper = two intersections of the fabric.

Photo by Charles W. Haralson.

Pattern Intoxication

MARION SCOULAR

See Color Plate 2.

Overall Size: 7¾" x 9".

MATERIALS

16" x 18" white 22-count hardanger
One skein black 6-strand embroidery cotton
#26 tapestry needle for patterns
#7 crewel needle for outlines

DIRECTIONS

Baste a line from top to bottom on the fabric to mark the center. Using the prick-and-pounce method, transfer the pattern to the fabric, matching the center of the hurricane glass with the basted line. Stretch the fabric taut on a rotating frame. Find the center at the top of each glass. This is where you will begin each pattern. The easiest way to work is to complete the light pattern over the whole glass, then return and work the additional stitches on the overlap. Use single strand for all patterns.

When all the patterns are complete, work the outlines in single- or double-thread outline stitch, as indicated.

The patterns and outlines are worked in 310 (black) double-thread outline, except where noted in the sketch.

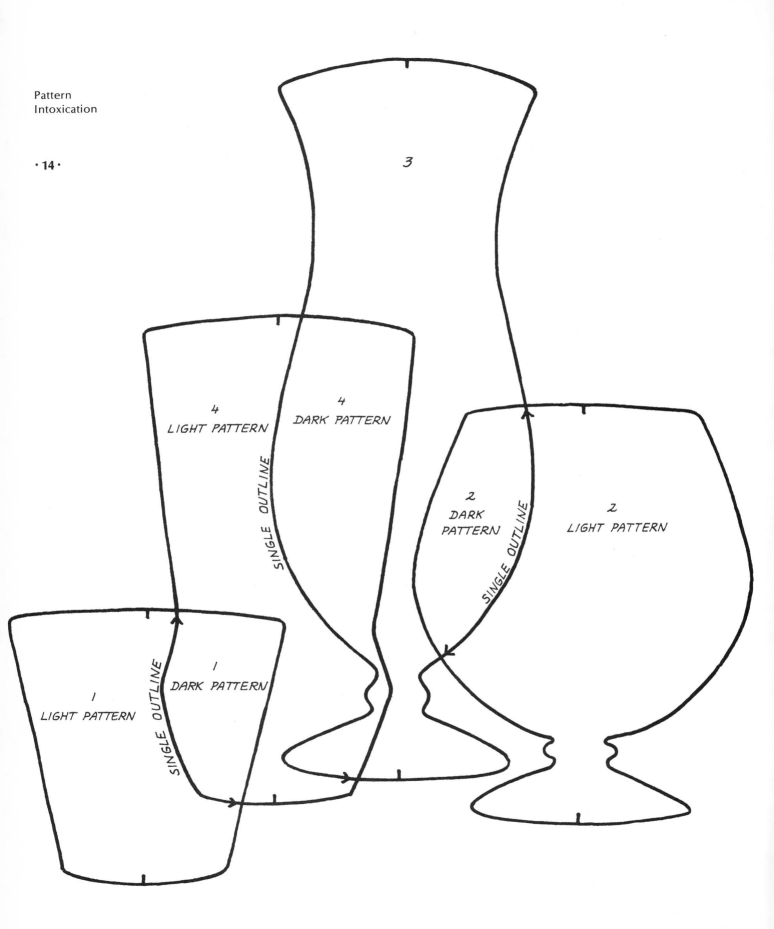

3

4
LIGHT PATTERN

4
DARK PATTERN

SINGLE OUTLINE

2
DARK
PATTERN

SINGLE OUTLINE

2
LIGHT PATTERN

1
LIGHT PATTERN

SINGLE OUTLINE

1
DARK PATTERN

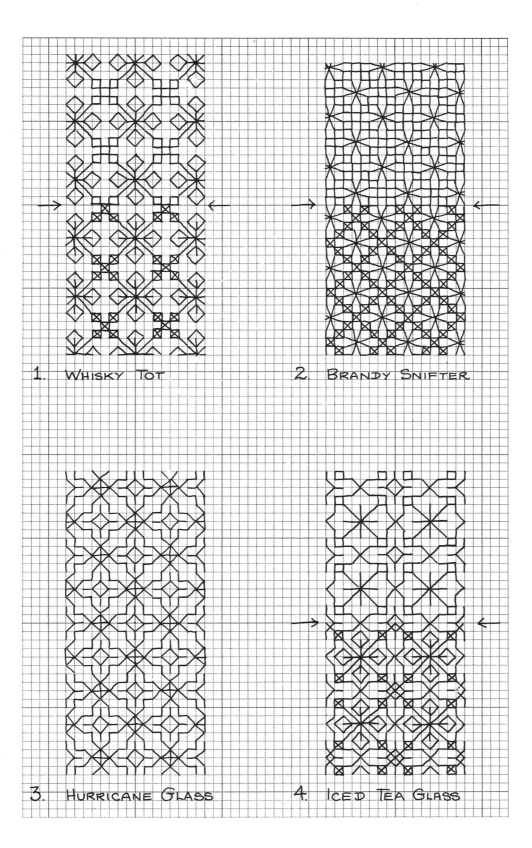

1. WHISKY TOT

2. BRANDY SNIFTER

3. HURRICANE GLASS

4. ICED TEA GLASS

A Night on the Tiles

MARION SCOULAR

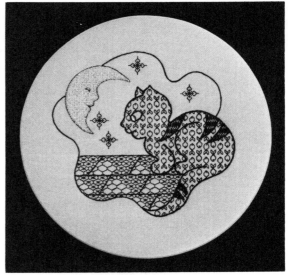

Overall Size: 7" diameter; 12" framed.

MATERIALS

14-inch square of gray 22-count hardanger
6 yards silver, D.M.C. fil Argent, 40-meter spool, fine
One skein black 6-strand embroidery cotton
#26 tapestry needle for patterns
#7 crewel needle for outlines

DIRECTIONS

Using the prick-and-pounce method, transfer the design to the fabric, trying to keep the roof line on the grain of the fabric. Stretch the fabric taut on a 10-inch hoop or mount it on a frame.

Outlines are worked after all the patterns are completed. Work the metal-thread pattern and outline last.

Use the backstitch for patterns 1, 2, 3, and 4, working with a single strand of D.M.C. embroidery cotton. Use double strand for the darning (4) and satin stitch (S.S.). On the tiles, if you will omit the star from several diamonds in the bottom left-hand corner of each tile, it will give the appearance of shading. Place several stars in the sky at random.

Number 3 pattern is to be stitched at random in the sky as stars, at the embroiderer's whim. Use number 5 pattern for the moon.

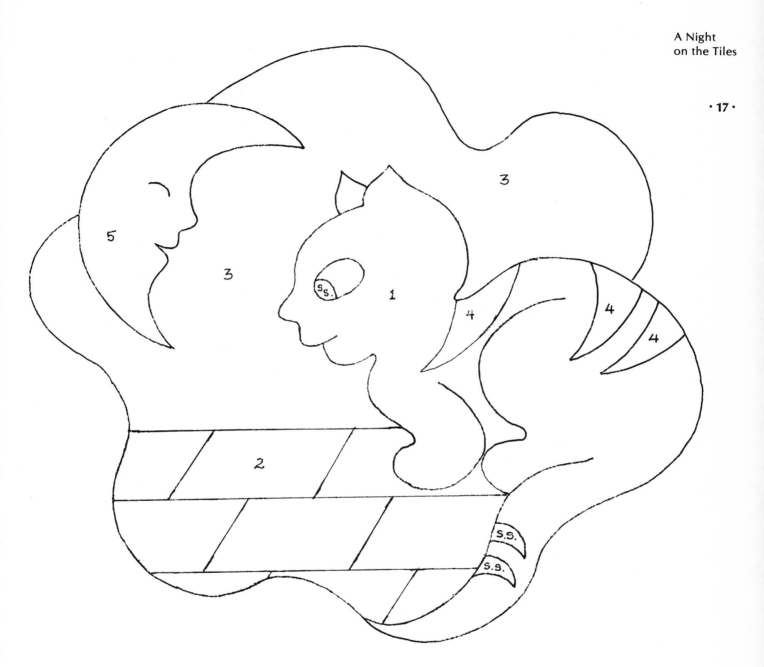

Position of Patterns

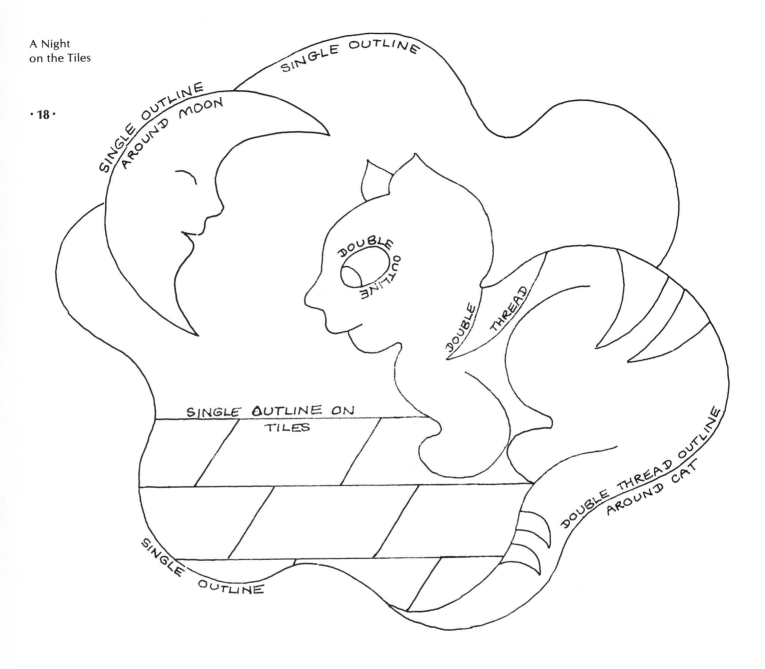

SINGLE OUTLINE

SINGLE OUTLINE
AROUND MOON

DOUBLE
OUTLINE

DOUBLE THREAD

SINGLE OUTLINE ON
TILES

SINGLE OUTLINE

DOUBLE THREAD OUTLINE
AROUND CAT

Outlines (Note the double-thread outline around the cat's stripes;
tail stripes and pupil of the eye are worked in satin stitch.)

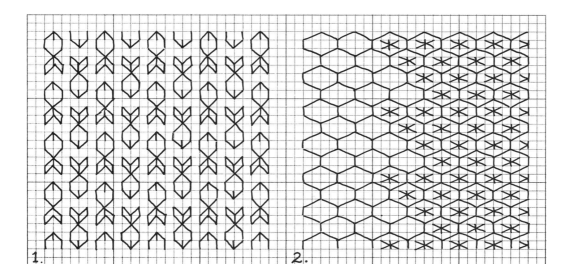

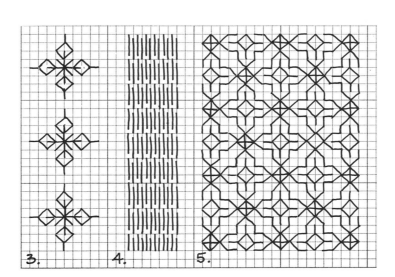

One square of the graph paper = two intersections of the fabric.

Pulled Thread and Assisi Embroidery

JANE D. ZIMMERMAN

Photo by Jane D. Zimmerman.

See Color Plate 3.

Overall Size: 12" x 12".

DIRECTIONS

This design is worked on #20 even-weave linen. The Assisi area is outlined in a double row of backstitch and its motif in double running stitch, both in a dark value of embroidery floss. The background of the motif is then filled with basic cross-stitch, in a medium dark or medium value. The cross-stitch and double running-stitch pattern of the border are worked in this same value. All stitches that are over two fabric threads in length are worked in four plies of floss.

The pulled-thread stitches can be worked in pearl cotton #8 or in a linen embroidery thread, the latter to be of the same thickness or thinner than the threads of the fabric.

Working hint: All the flat counted work—cross-stitch and double running—should be executed before the pulled work is begun in an area. Take care not to carry the embroidery thread behind an area that will subsequently be executed in pulled work.

Stitch Detail in Close-up

Pulled Thread and Florentine Embroidery

JANE D. ZIMMERMAN

See Color Plate 4.

Photo by Jane D. Zimmerman.

Overall Size: 9¾" x 13".

DIRECTIONS

This design, using an adaptation of a carnation motif from an eighteenth-century English Florentine pattern, is worked on #20 even-weave linen. All the Florentine work, using a 4-2 step, is executed in eight plies of embroidery floss. The pulled-thread stitches can be worked in pearl cotton #8 or in a linen embroidery thread, the latter to be of the same thickness or thinner than the threads of the fabric.

Working hint: All the Florentine work should be executed before the pulled work is begun in an area. Take care not to carry the embroidery thread used in the Florentine work behind an area that will subsequently be executed in pulled work.

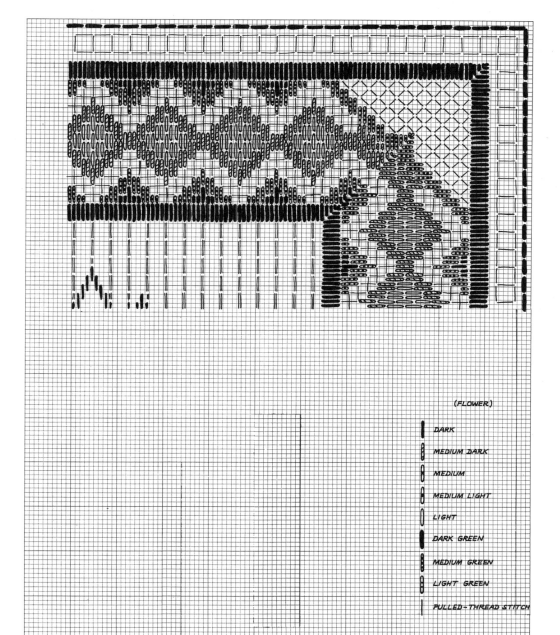

(FLOWER)

DARK

MEDIUM DARK

MEDIUM

MEDIUM LIGHT

LIGHT

DARK GREEN

MEDIUM GREEN

LIGHT GREEN

PULLED-THREAD STITCH

Border Stitch Detail in Close-up

Squirrel on Branch

AUDREY FRANCINI

Photo by Loy Westbury.

See Color Plate 5.

Overall Size: 6½" x 10¼".

DIRECTIONS

This design is worked in lightweight crewel yarn and floss on blue British satin.

Stitch Key

1: Chain Stitch	10: Laid work
2: Whipped chain stitch	11: Simple trellis
3: Twisted chain stitch	12: Chinese knot stitch
4: Soft shading	13: Bullion knot stitch
5: Closed fly stitch	14: French knot stitch
6: Fishbone stitch	15: Needle weaving
7: Outline stitch	16: Detached buttonhole bars
8: Stem stitch	17: Turkey work
9: Detatched fly stitch	18: Satin stitch

On the design sketch, the stitch number is underlined.

Color and Thread Key
B 1, 2, 3: Blue
P 1, 2: Purple
R 1, 2, 3, 4: Rose
Y 1, 2: Yellow
YG 1, 2, 3: Yellow-green
OG 2, 3: Olive green
Br 1, 2, 3, 4: Brown
W: White
GF: Green floss
RF: Red floss
WF: White floss
BlF: Black floss
GrF 1, 2, 3: Gray floss
BF 1, 3: Blue floss
PF 1, 3: Purple floss

The lowest number following the color designation equals the lightest shade. Follow the picture for placement of shades for butterfly, bird, squirrel, and rose-colored flowers.

Design sketches for Squirrel on Branch follow, on pages 28 and 29.

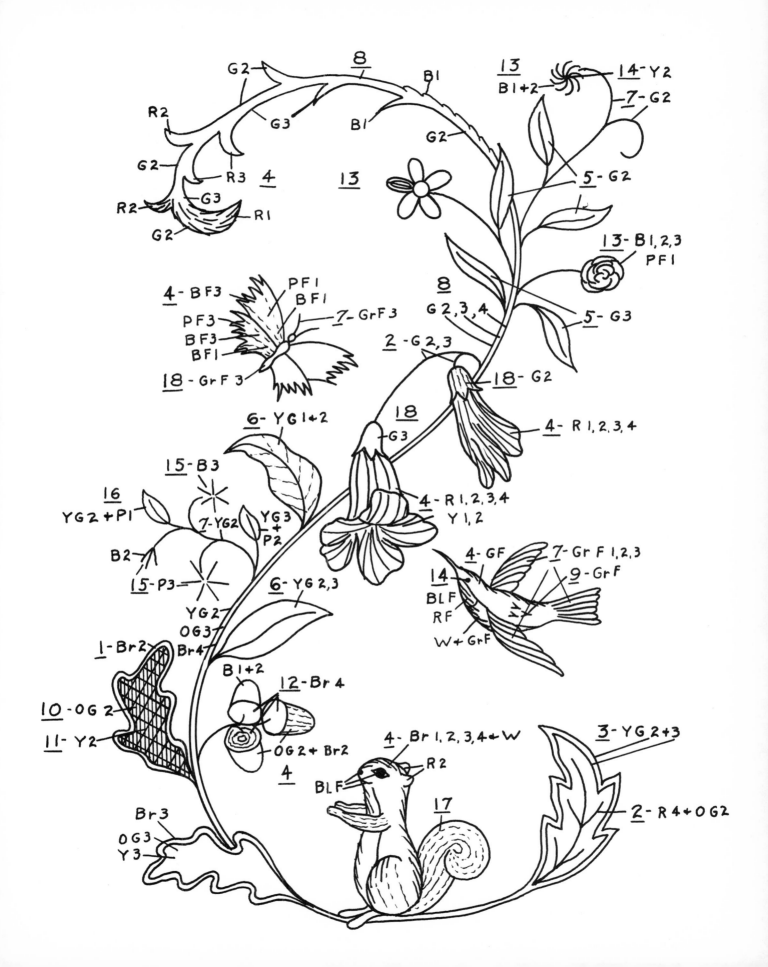

Floral

AUDREY FRANCINI

Photo by Loy Westbury.

See Color Plate 6.

Overall Size: 5" x 7½".

DIRECTIONS

This design is worked in lightweight crewel yarn on linen twill.

Stitch Key

1: Chain stitch
2: Whipped chain stitch
3: Close buttonhole stitch
4: Detached buttonhole bars
5: Whipped back stitch
6: Whipped outline stitch
7: Stem stitch
8: Raised stem stitch
9: Closed fly stitch
10: Fishbone stitch
11: Soft shading

12: Circular whipped spider stitch
13: Horizontal spider stitch
14: Crescent spider stitch
15: French knot stitch
16: Bullion knot stitch
17: Seed stitch
18: Overlaid filler
19: Checkerboard filler
20: Scroll stitch
21: Couched leaf stitch
22: Satin stitch

On the design sketch, the stitch number is underlined.

Color Key
B 1, 2, 3: Blue
YG 1, 2, 3: Yellow-green
G 1, 2, 3: Green
C 1, 2, 3, 4: Coral
Y 1, 2, 3, 4: Yellow

The lowest number following the color designation equals the lightest shade.

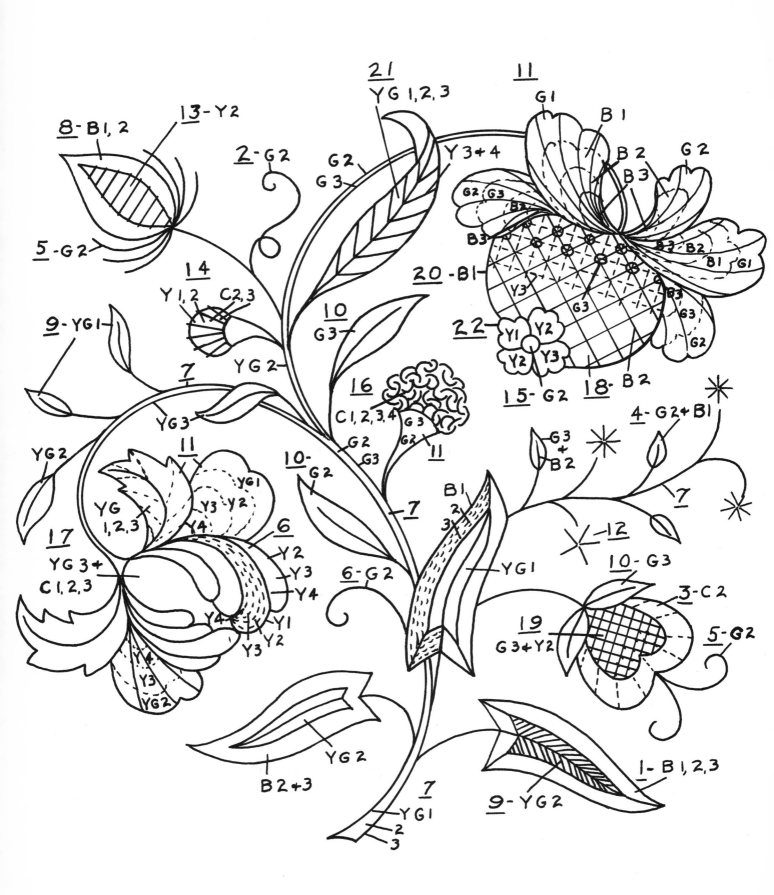

Bouquet

A U D R E Y   F R A N C I N I

See Color Plate 7.

Overall Size: 7¾" x 7¾".

DIRECTIONS

This design is worked in crewel yarn, floss, and perle cotton, on brown British satin.

Stitch Key

1: Split stitch
2: Coral knot stitch
3: Closed fly stitch
4: Slanted satin stitch
5: Satin stitch
6: Bullion knot stitch
7: Needle weaving

8: Soft shading
9: Straight stitch
10: Laid work couched with trellis
11: Laid work with pattern couching
12: Laid work with bricked couching
13: Whipped outline or backstitch

On the design sketch, the stitch number is underlined.

Color Key

Y 1, 2, 3, 4: Yellow
P 1, 2, 3: Purple
B 1, 2: Blue
G 1, 2, 3: Green
OG 1, 2, 3: Olive green
YG 1, 2, 3: Yellow-green
Br 3: Brown
YP: Yellow perle

BP 1, 2: Blue perle
BL: Blue linen
WF: White floss
GF: Green floss
BF 1, 2, 3: Blue floss
PF 1, 2: Purple floss
BrF: Brown floss

The lowest number following the color designation equals the lightest shade.

BOUQUET

Padding the vase. Cut three pieces of blue felt, one very slightly larger than the vase, one ¼ inch (6 mm.) smaller than the vase, and one ½ inch (12 mm.) smaller than the vase. Mark the couching lines on the largest. Center and sew the smallest piece in place over the marked design, using small stabbing stitches at right angles to the edge of the felt with a matching color thread. Center and sew down the medium-size piece in the same manner, then the largest piece, so that its edges match those of the design. Lay the linen thread over this, couching with blue wool on the lines.

Templates for Cutting Felt Padding for Vase

Milkweed pods. Use a variety of greens and a little brown with alternating rows of split and coral knot stitches to create a textured appearance. Rows should follow the contours of the pod. Slightly heavier yarn can be used on these two areas to give them added weight.

Thistles. Work in several values of yarn, then highlight them with the purple floss.

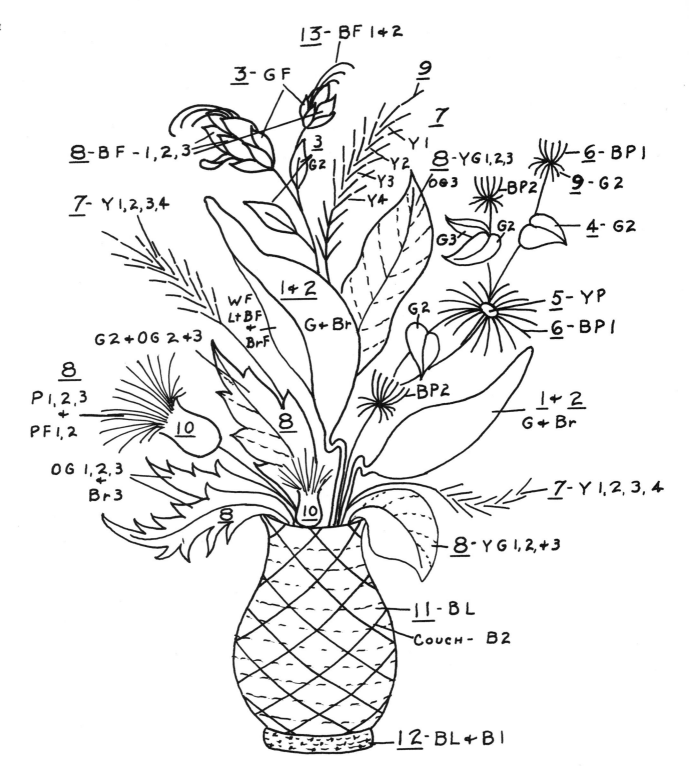

13 - BF 1+2

3 - GF

9

7

8 - BF - 1,2,3

3
G2

Y1

Y2

Y3

Y4

8 - YG 1,2,3
OG3

6 - BP1

9 - G2

BP2

G2

4 - G2

7 - Y 1,2,3,4

G3

G2

5 - YP

6 - BP1

WF
Lt BF
+
Br F

1+2

G + Br

G2 + OG 2+3

8

P 1,2,3
+
PF 1,2

10

8

BP2

1+2

G + Br

OG 1,2,3
+
Br 3

8

10

7 - Y 1,2,3,4

8 - YG 1,2,+3

11 - BL

Couch - B2

12 - BL + B1

Flower Basket

BARBARA EYRE

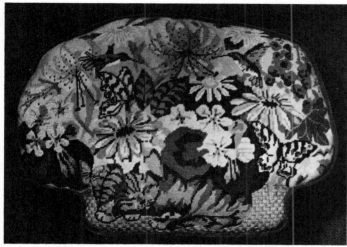

Photo by Harold Pratt.

See Color Plate 8.

Overall Size: 19" x 14".

DIRECTIONS

In stitching, use encroaching Gobelin stitch for the lilies and geraniums (A) and basket-filling stitch for the basket (B). The remainder of the design is in tent stitch or basketweave. The butterflies and the hummingbirds are worked in either silk or mouline.

Color Key

1: Black	16: Dark brown
2: White	17: Light lettuce green
3: Light gray	18: Medium lettuce green
4: Medium gray	19: Light lemon yellow
5: Dark gray	20: Medium lemon yellow
6: Light green	21: Light blue
7: Medium green	22: Medium blue
8: Dark green	23: Dark blue
9: Light pink	24: Light orange
10: Medium pink	25: Medium orange
11: Light yellow	26: Dark orange
12: Medium yellow	27: Kelly green
13: Red-brown	28: Dark red
14: Light brown	29: Light aqua
15: Medium brown	

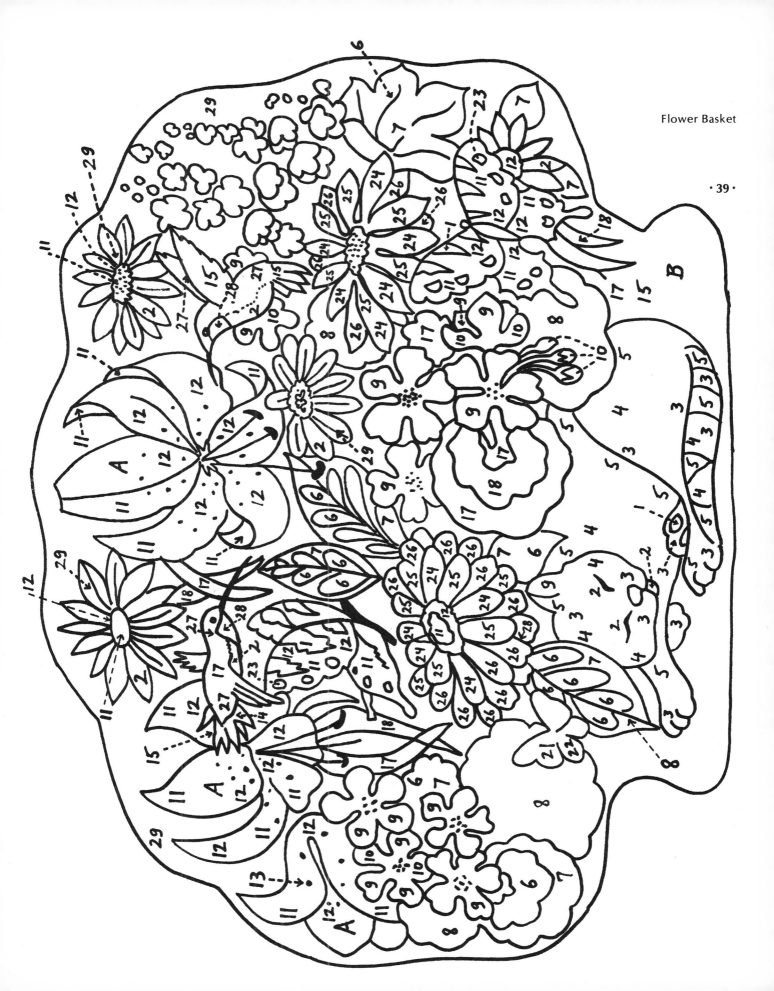

Flower Basket

· 39 ·

Squirrel

B A R B A R A   E Y R E

See Color Plate 9.

Photo by Harold Pratt.

Overall Size: 12" x 14".

DIRECTIONS

In stitching, those sections of the design sketch labeled "A" should be done in French knots, those labeled "B" in long and short stitch. The remainder of the design should be done in diagonal tent stitch or basketweave.

Color Key

1: White
2: Black
3: Light green
4: Medium green
5: Dark green
6: Light aqua
7: Citrus green
8: Medium yellow
9: Dark yellow
10: Copper
11: Red-brown
12: Light gray
13: Medium gray
14: Dark gray
15: Cream
16: Gray-brown
17: Medium blue—background

The dots on head and back are worked free form—in cream and medium gray—using tent stitch. The eye is done in black silk.

Christmas Wreath

BARBARA EYRE

See Color Plate 10.

Photo by Harold Pratt.

Overall Size: 20" in diameter.

MATERIALS

Wools (silk or mouline)
Gold metallic thread

DIRECTIONS

All the bodies are done in tent stitch, all the teeth in Gobelin. All the stars are done in tent stitch with gold metallic thread; the stars are attached to the poles by gold threads overlaying the worked background. The background is jacquard stitch. Stitches for special parts of the animals, beginning at the top of the wreath, follow.

Left-hand Beaver
Slanting mosaic stitch—jacket (pearl buttons on jacket)
Kalem stitch (done in two directions)—scarf
Oblique Gobelin stitch—both beaver tails

Middle Beaver
Split Gobelin stitch—sweater
Upright Gobelin stitch—cuffs
Encroaching Gobelin stitch—book
Gobelin stitch (worked sideways)—binding of book

Right-hand Beaver
Jacket is worked in tent stitch in a check or a plaid

Raccoon
Turkey work—earmuffs
Smyrna cross-stitch—sweater
Satin stitch worked sideways—tail

Squirrel
Overlaid free form—tail
Cross-stitch—scarf
Encroaching Gobelin stitch—inside ears
Encroaching Gobelin stitch—book
Satin stitch—bookbinding

Rabbit
Mosaic stitch—sweater
Encroaching Gobelin stitch—inside ears
Cross-stitch—neck and bottom of sweater
Gobelin stitch—cuffs

Moles (left and right)
Czar stitch—scarves
Turkey work—ends of scarves

Left-hand Mouse
Encroaching Gobelin stitch—inside ears and tail
Upright cross-stitch—jacket (done in silk or mouline)
Cross-stitch—dots on scarf

Right-hand Mouse
Scotch stitch—coat (done in silk or mouline)
Encroaching Gobelin stitch—tail and inside ears

Small Foxes
Brick stitch—mittens
Long and short stitch—tails

Large Fox
Gobelin stitch (done in silk or mouline)—scarf
Kalem stitch—jacket (real leather patch appliquéd to elbow of jacket)
Turkey work—tail

Color Key
 1: Black
 2: White
 3: Light gray
 4: Medium gray
 5: Dark gray
 6: Light yellow
 7: Medium yellow
 8: Light red-brown
 9: Medium red-brown
10: Dark red-brown
11: Light golden brown
12: Medium golden brown
13: Dark golden brown
14: Light pink
15: Medium pink
16: Royal blue
17: Medium hunter green
18: Dark hunter green
19: Tan appliquéd suede
20: Gold metallic thread
21: Red
22: Yellow-green
23: Orange
24: Maroon
25: Aqua-blue
26: Medium blue
27: Dark blue
28: Green-maroon-cream check

Design sketches for Christmas Wreath follow, on pages 46 and 47.

Basket of Flowers
White Work

MARGARET LUNT

Photo by Chet Brickett.

Overall Size: Design 9" x 9". Background size as desired.

Stitch Key
A: Back-stitched chain
B: Cross-stitch over four threads
C: Foursquare stitch over four threads
D: Ripple stitch
E: Pulled satin over four threads
F: Coral stitch
G: Backstitch
H: Square eyelet over eight threads
J: Buttonhole
K: Zigzag over four single threads

L: Zigzag over four double threads
M: Greek cross filling—close—diagonal
N: Thicket filling
O: Window filling worked in vertical rows
P: Step stitch
Q: Single faggot over three threads
R: Foursquare filling over two threads
S: Straight stitches
T: Square eyelet over four threads
U: Whipped chain

A
A
A
A
J
U
U
KLK
R
U
U
G
M
U
U
P
KLK
U
A
U
U
Q
T
T
U
F
U
T
U
G
S
H
U
U
U
O
T
U
U
T
N
T
A
A
T
A
A
A
E
A
D
A
A
B
C
B
A
E
A

Court Lady with Mirror

Photo by Bob Talley.

MARY ASCOT

See Color Plate 11.

Overall Size: 17⅛" x 31⅝". The height of the figure from top of veil to bottom of skirt is 27¼".

This design is one of a number of such figures incised on stone slabs to decorate the tomb of a Chinese nobleman. They date from about 700 A.D. and are now in the Shensi Museum in China.

The hanging has been especially designed to be worked in shades of any one fairly neutral color and one strong contrast color, in order to approximate the subtle feeling of the old rolled Oriental scrolls. The original was worked in camel browns with a light beige background shade. Chinese lacquer red was used for contrast. Other equally appropriate families might be the beige-browns, bronze-greens, or pure golds.

Stitch Key
A: French basketweave stitch
B: Cross-stitch
C: Chain stitch
D: Checker stitch
E: Long cross-stitch
F: Diamond leaf stitch
G: Vertical rows of tent stitch
H: French knots

DIRECTIONS

In the following Directions, "1" represents the darkest shade and "7" the lightest.

Figure Outline

Outline in tent stitch the entire figure in the darkest shade, 1, with a double line on the collar. Where it is necessary to keep a solid line (on eyebrows, hands, nose, chin, etc.), turn your canvas 90 degrees and reverse the slant of your stitch from / to \.

Neckband and Collar

Neckband: Shade 4
Double line: Shade 1
Chest section: Cross-stitch, shade 3
Inside of collar: Shade 2
Collar: Chain stitch (start at point A and follow contour of curve), shade 3

Hairdo

Bottom part: Shade 1
Beehive part (all four sections): Shade 3

Face and Neck

Eyes: Solid shade 1
Face and neck: Shade 3

Headdress

Fill in question-mark shape with shade 3. Then put in two rows of basketweave, shade 6 (your background shade), on either side of the question mark to form a base for the dots. Embroider regularly spaced French knots in a dark shade of D.M.C. floss on each side, using spacing as indicated in the color photo. Measure visually rather than by trying to place them exactly on every second or third stitch.

Flowers in Headdress

Solid in shade 1, except for one stitch in the center in shade 6

Veil on Headdress

The veil on the headdress is in four sections, D-7 (see photo). The veil is worked in checker stitch with cotton floss. Some of the canvas threads show in the finished design. This is intentional.

Sleeves

Lower sleeves: Shade 3 (same as chest section of dress)
Upper sleeves and bodice of dress to waistband: Shade 4 for large cross-stitch, tied; filler, small cross-stitch, in shade 2

Sash

The sash is in shade 3.

Skirt

Basic skirt: Diamond leaf stitch, shade 2. (After finishing the diamond leaf stitch, do a long stitch in the spaces using one strand of shade 4.)
Bottom inside of skirt: Diamond leaf stitch, shade 1; long stitch, shade 3

Clogs

Work in vertical stripes, alternating shades 1 and 5.

Hands

The hands are in shade 5.

Mirror

Outer ring and handle: Shade 2
Inner circle: Shade 3

Work two rows of plain basketweave around both figure and mirror and contrast color designs, shade 6.

Background

Pavilion boxes stitch: Shade 6. Border is a continuation of this stitch with the horizontal stitches worked in shade 6 and the diagonals worked in shade 2. Lay your horizontal stitches first, then put in all the diagonals.
Begin at the top, center line of canvas, and work consistently. On the top horizontal row, the original has thirty-three diamond boxes across the plain background area, 2½ boxes on top and bottom borders, 3 boxes on each side border (see photo). If you wish to use a different background stitch, mark off with sewing thread an area equal to the plain area in the original (14⅜" x 29¼"), center your first stitch unit, and make sure your units are worked symmetrically.

Design sketches for Court Lady with Mirror follow, on pages 54 and 55.

Court Lady
with Mirror

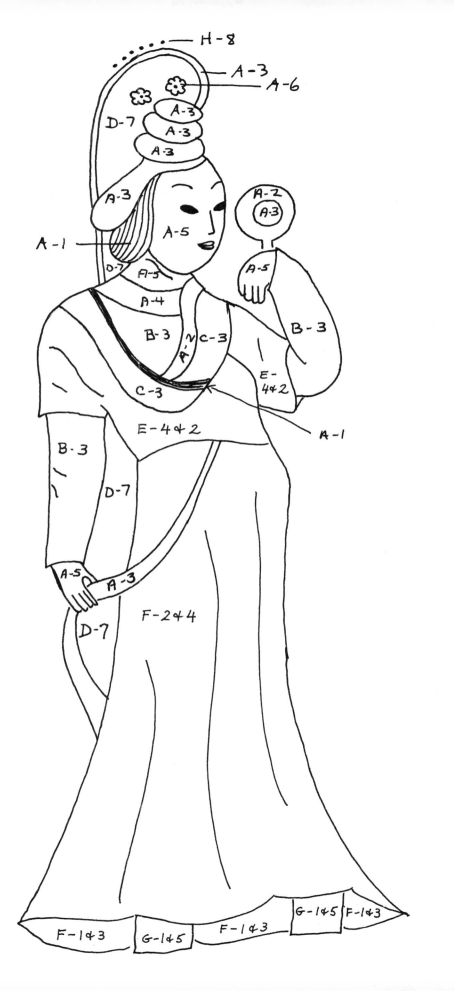

Horses' Heads

GAY ANN ROGERS

Photo by Gay Ann Rogers.

See Color Plate 12.

Overall Size: See below.

The graph for the color wheel of Horses' Heads will make either a wall hanging on 18-mesh canvas or a circular rug on 10-mesh canvas.

The graph measures 452 threads in diameter. To make a wall hanging, cut and bind a piece of 18-mesh canvas 30" x 30" for a finished piece of needlepoint approximately 25" in diameter. To make a circular rug, cut and bind a piece of 10-mesh canvas 50" x 50" for a finished piece of needlepoint approximately 45" in diameter.

The graph for Horses' Heads is in eleven pieces. To put the graph together, match the letters at the edges of each separate graph piece (see below):

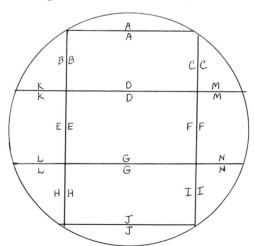

DIRECTIONS

To stitch the project, find and mark the center of the canvas to correspond to the center of the graph. Begin to stitch at the center of the canvas. Stitch the black outlines first.

Stitch and Color Key
◪ Tent stitch, black
Ⓢ Cross-stitch, yellow
⊞ Slanting Gobelin stitch, yellow-orange
⊞ Milanese stitch, orange
⊠ Rice stitch, red
◩ Scotch stitch, hot pink
◺ Jacquard stitch, light pink
ⓒ Hungarian stitch, dusty pink
◹ Cross-stitch, light purple
◉ St. George and St. Andrew stitch, blue
☐ Moorish stitch, light blue
◙ Large and upright cross-stitch, green
☐ Oriental stitch, white (for background)
Use tent stitch for the horses' eyes and nostrils.

Materials and directions for finishing the piece follow:

MATERIALS
Suggested backing: natural kettlecloth
One tube black Fawcett linen warp
One 36-inch metal hoop (available in most weaving stores)
1 ounce each light blue and yellow-orange yarn
2 ounces each hot pink and dusty pink yarn
3 ounces each orange, yellow, green, and blue yarn
4 ounces each red and light purple yarn
5 ounces light pink yarn

1. Block the finished piece of needlepoint.
2. Cut the backing to match size of the needlepoint. With right sides basted together, sew the backing to the needlepoint. Leave opening large enough to turn right sides out. After turning, baste the opening closed.
3. Wrap the hoop with black linen.
4. Suspend the needlepoint in the center of the hoop with black linen at the fourteen points indicated in Diagram 1 (see pages 72–74 for diagrams) by using the method illustrated in Diagrams 2, 3, 4, and 5. *Note:* Wrap three times vertically before beginning to wrap horizontally.

5. Using the photo of the finished hanging as a guide for color placement, mount four strands of each color with lark's-head knots (Diagrams 6, 7, and 8). Repeat pattern of alternating square knots until the strip is long enough to reach from needlepoint to hoop with slight tension (Diagrams 9, 10, and 11).

6. Secure the ends to hoop by tying each strand with double half-hitch knots (Diagram 12).

7. Check the photo of the finished hanging. Where macramé extends outside the hoop, use the pattern of square knots illustrated in Diagram 13. At the same time, work diagonal rows of double half-hitch knots as the finished hanging indicates, so that the rows of knots meet at points.

Top

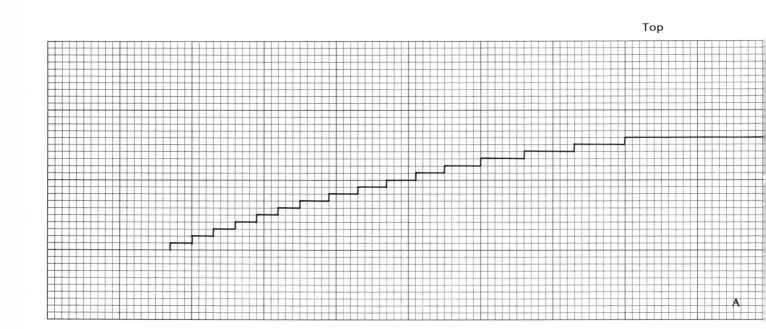

A

8. Make tassels with remaining yarn of each color. To make tassels, double-cut the yarn, double again (Diagram 14). Tie a strand of yarn around center of the doubled yarn (Diagrams 15 and 16). Tie a strand of yarn approximately one-third of the way down to form the tassel head; clip bottom of the tassel to desired length (Diagram 17). The light pink tassel from center point is largest; red and light purple tassels are slightly smaller; orange, yellow, green, and blue tassels are still smaller; smallest tassels hang from hot pink and dusty pink points.

9. Where illustrated in the photo of finished hanging, attach the tassels.

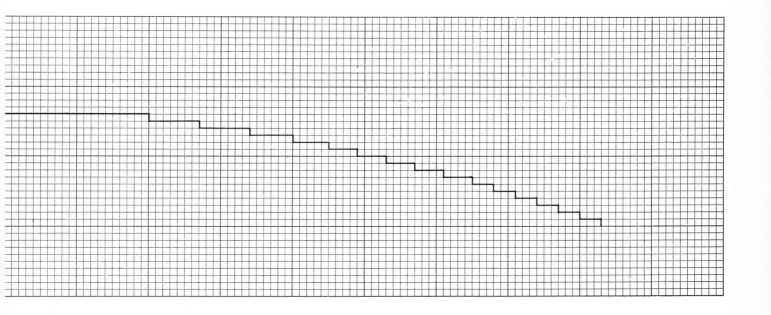

C

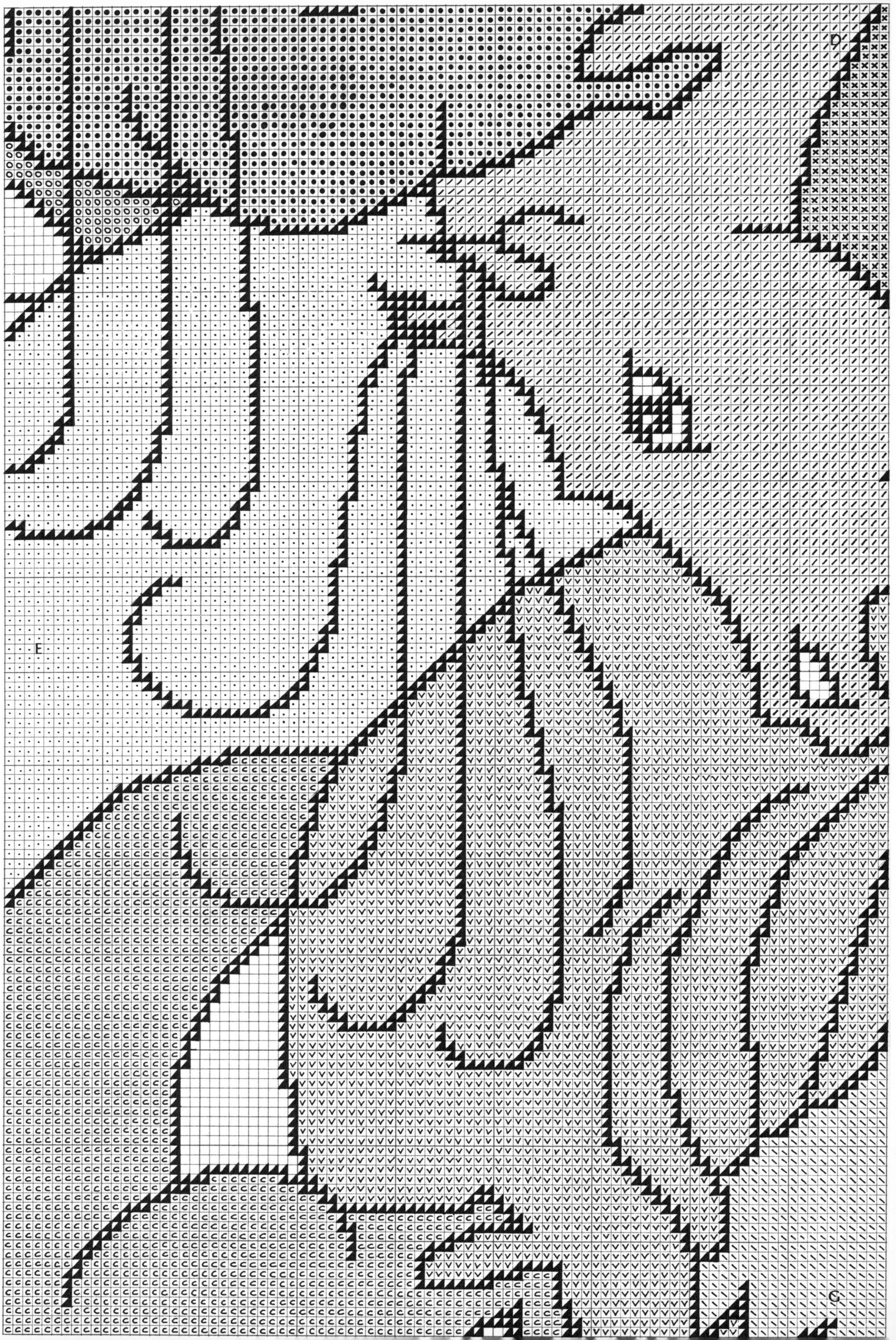
D
E
C

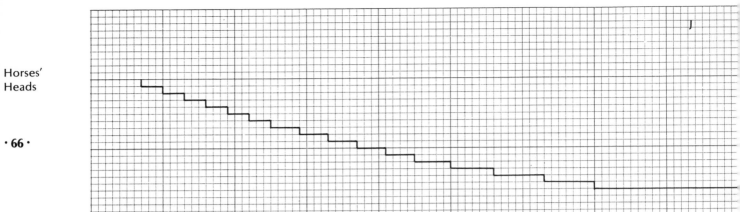

J

Bottom

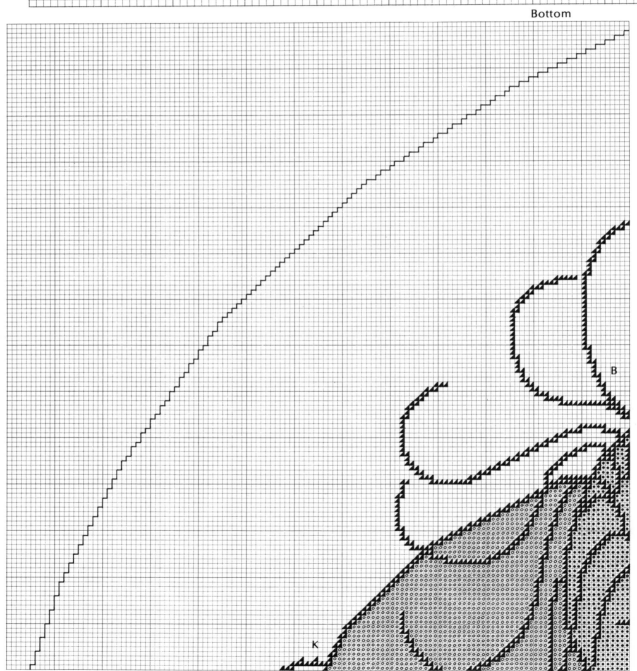

B

K

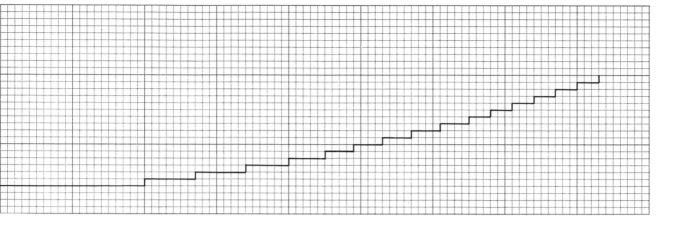

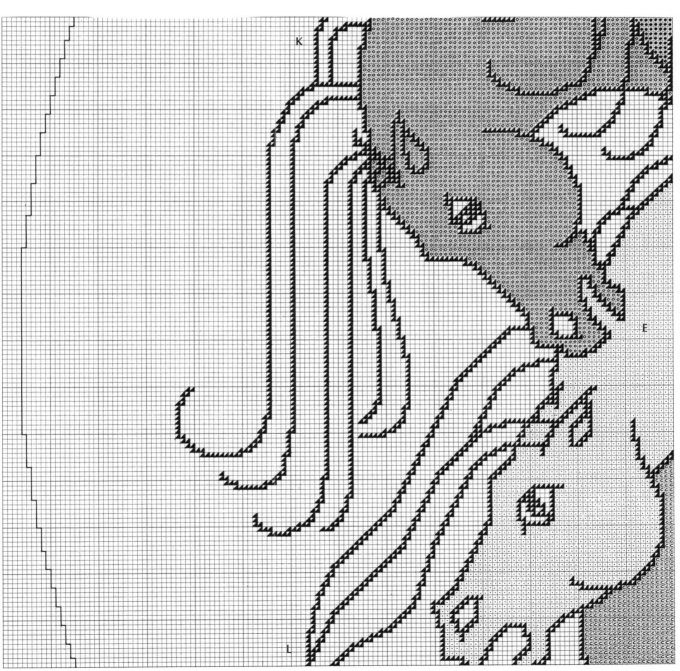

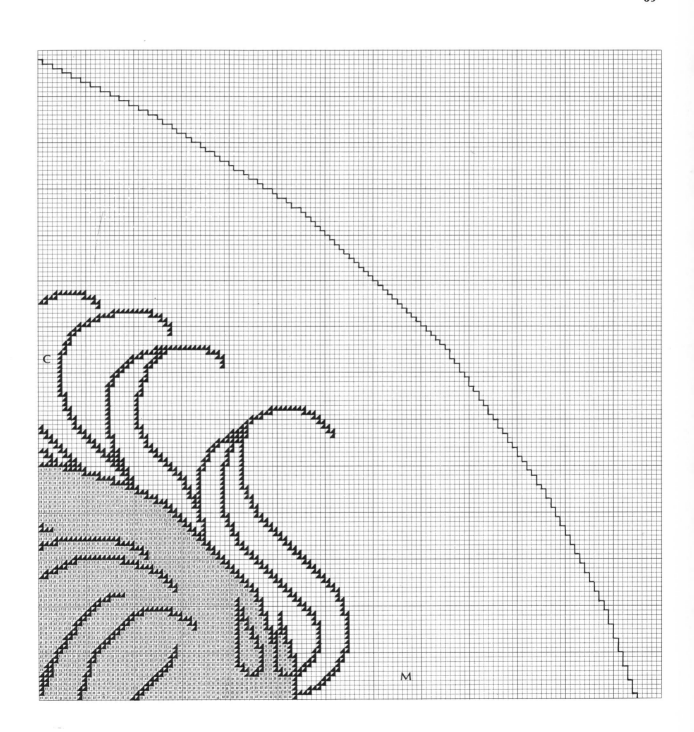

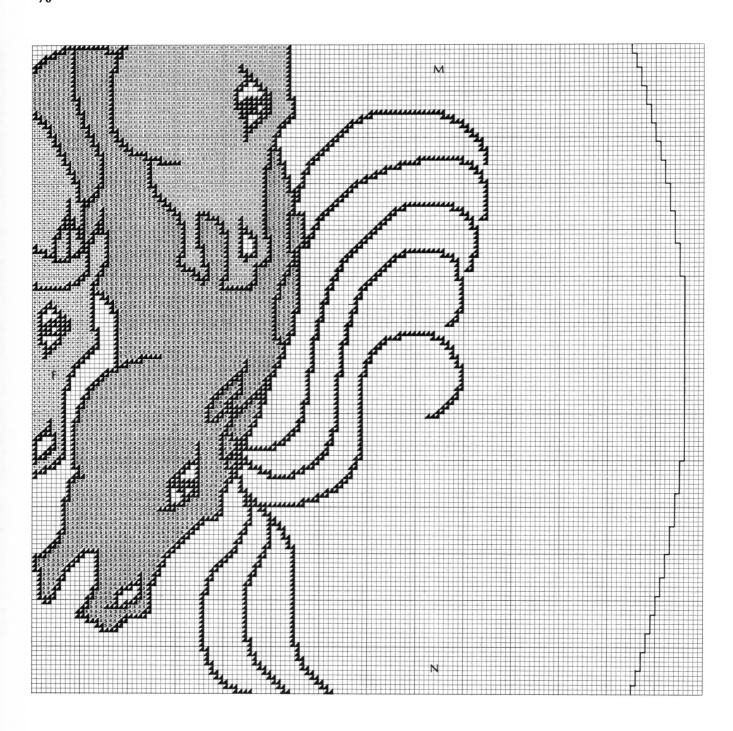

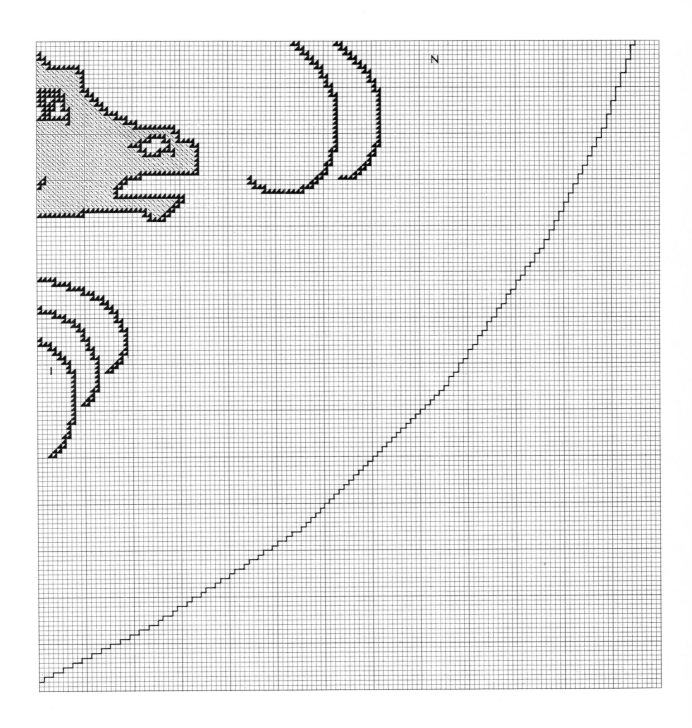

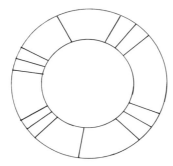

Diagram 1

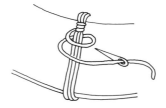

Diagram 4

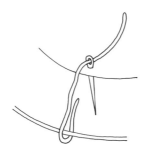

Diagram 2

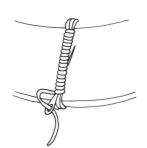

Diagram 5

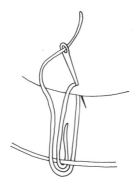

Diagram 3

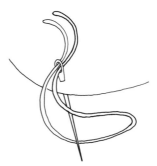

Diagram 6

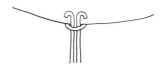

Diagram 7: Lark's-head Knot

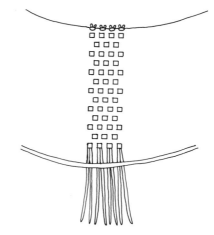

Diagram 11

Diagram 8

Diagram 9: Square Knot

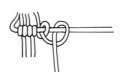

Diagram 12: Double Half-hitch Knot

Each box represents one square knot.

Diagram 10

Diagram 13

Diagram 14

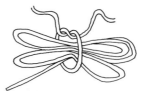

Diagram 15

Diagram 16

Diagram 17

Photo by Gay Ann Rogers.

Pottery

GAY ANN ROGERS

See Color Plate 13.

Overall Size: See below.

The graph for pottery measures 181 threads at its tallest point by 168 threads at its widest point. Cut and bind a piece of 12-mesh canvas 18″ x 17″ for a finished piece of needlepoint approximately 15″ x 14″.

DIRECTIONS

Find and mark the center of the canvas to correspond to the center of the graph. Begin to stitch at the center of the canvas. Stitch the black areas first.

Stitch and Color Key
◪ Tent stitch, black
⊠ Smyrna cross-stitch, brown
⊻ Tent stitch, light gray
⊡ Tent stitch, gray
⊡ Slanting Gobelin stitch, white
⊞ Smyrna cross-stitch, white
☑ Smyrna cross-stitch, light brown
☐ Tent stitch, white

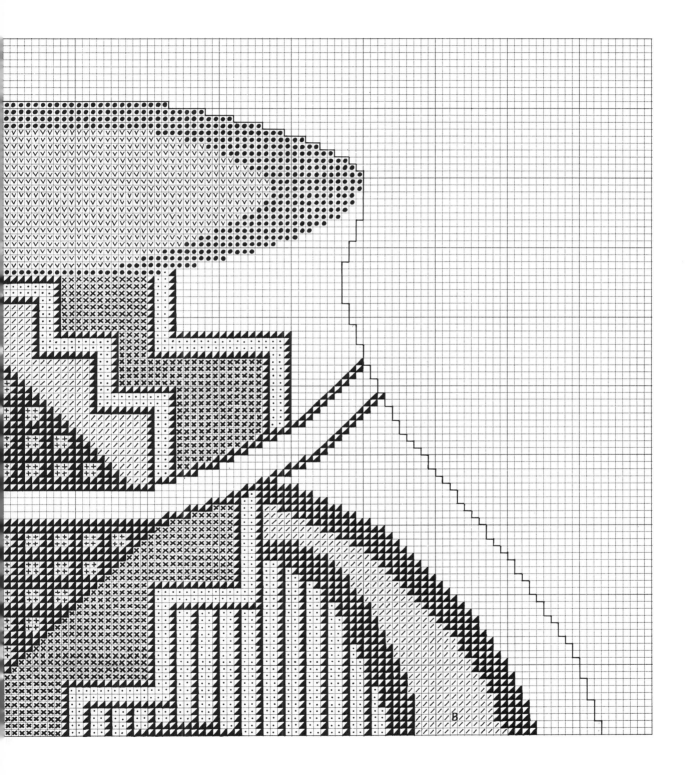

Bottom

Whelk

NELLIE BERGH

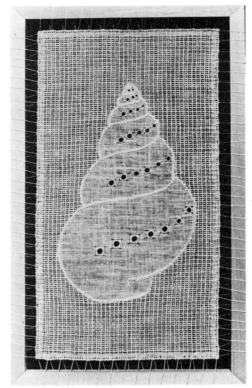

Photo by Philip Bergh.

Overall Size: Design 12". Fabric 18½" x 9¾". Frame 21" x 12¼" on the outside.

Whelk is an embroidered interpretation of a shell native to northern Japan. There are many beautiful shell shapes suitable for interpretation in this medium.

MATERIALS

Length of white even-weave linen, 26 threads to the inch
White tatting thread for the pulled-thread embroidery and for hemming
#3 white perle cotton for outlining the shell
#8 white perle cotton for the eyelets
#5 white perle cotton for lacing the finished embroidery into its frame

DIRECTIONS

Any delicate shell-like color can be used both for the background and the stitchery.

Fasten fabric into a stretcher frame 22″ x 14″. Make certain that the warp and weft threads are parallel to the frame.

Make a 1-inch grid on a sheet of paper 13″ x 8″ and copy the shell diagram square by square. Cut out the drawing of the shell and center it on fabric. Pin securely. With black sewing thread, using running stitches, sew closely around the paper. Put long tailor's tacks through paper and cloth at the center of each eyelet. Baste your four frame lines. In the original, the background area is 17¼″ x 8⅝″.

The background is cobbler filling. However, any pulled-thread stitch could be used. Work up to the basted outline of the shell. Outline the shell with alternating stem stitch, over two threads, on a vertical or horizontal line.

The eyelets vary in size. Reading from right to left, top to bottom, the thread count is as follows:

4 and 4
4, 4, and 6
4, 6, 6, and 8
6, 8, 8, 10, and 10
8, 8, 10, 10, 12, and 12
10, 10, 12, 12, 14, 14, and 14

The hem is ¼″, folded on a thread, with its corners mitered.
Press fabric facedown on several layers of toweling with a steam iron.
Measure the piece accurately to the sixteenth of an inch and have a framer construct a frame of ¾″ x ¾″ wood with the outer dimensions 2½″ longer and wider than the embroidery. Wax the frame. Lace your embroidery into frame (see photo).

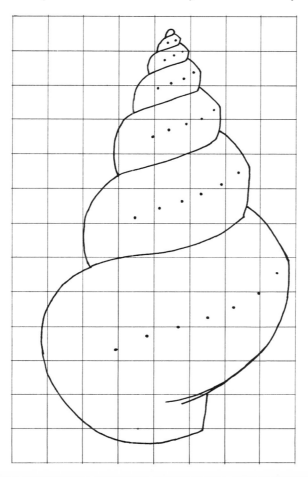

Bird of Paradise

ELSA T. COSE

Photo by David Feisner.

See Color Plate 14.

Overall Size: 6″ high x 4¼″ wide.

MATERIALS

4 yards #8 Japanese gold
2 yards gold crinkle, fine
1 yard silver braid, ⅛″ wide
12-inch strand gold check purl
One skein orange silk floss
One skein yellow silk floss
One skein blue silk floss
One spool gold silk sewing thread
One spool gray silk sewing thread
One package #10 crewel needles
One package #9 crewel needles
#18 chenille needle
#20 chenille needle
12″ x 12″ piece of linen or muslin for backing
12″ x 12″ piece of ground fabric
Stretcher frame

PREPARATION

    A. Stretch the backing fabric on the frame.

    B. Attach the ground fabric to the backing.

    C. Trace the design onto the fabric, using dressmaker's carbon.

    D. Go over all traced lines with stitching. Use a single strand of yellow floss around the flower petals in split stitch, blue floss on leaves. Go over all other lines in running stitch, using waxed silk sewing thread.

DIRECTIONS

    1. All the leaves are satin stitch in blue floss; the flowers are in yellow satin stitch. The stitch direction is indicated on the pattern by double lines. French knots are in orange floss.

    2. The wings and head are all worked at once. Begin at the upper wing's tip. Pull one strand of #8 gold through to the back using a #20 chenille needle. Sink a second strand of gold ¼" in from the tip, so the wing looks tapered. Lay the two strands on the line, couching with waxed silk sewing thread. At the beak, turn sharply, and follow the line around to the tip of the lower wing. Sink the outside strand of gold at the tip, the other strand ¼" before. The second row begins at the second line on the upper wing, meeting the first row near the curve. Lay alongside the first row, bricking the stitches. Near the lower wing's tip, taper ends again when sinking. Continue in this manner, filling in the center of the head area with short rows, if necessary. Couch the beak with several stitches of orange floss. The eye is blue floss.

    3. For the tail feathers, fold a length of #8 gold, and couch with waxed silk sewing thread, with the first stitch over the loop at the far end of the tail feather. Gold will be laid single strand around the curve; then two strands will meet, and couching stitches will go over both strands along the line to the body. At the body, cut, leaving 1-inch tails, and pull the tails through to the back with a chenille needle. The two small tail feathers are begun at the body, couching a single strand of gold. Follow the line, go around the loop, cut, and sink, completing the loop.

    4. Lay a single strand of crinkle around the edge of each tail feather, couching with silk sewing thread. The end of the crinkle should be pulled through to the back. Add curls to the feathers and the top of the head with the crinkle.

    5. Cut the check purl into bits of varying lengths. Using waxed silk sewing thread, thread the purl and sew into place like beads on lines of the body.

    6. Lay the silver braid on the stem lines, sewing into place with gray silk sewing thread, waxed. Make stabbing stitches into the braid, alternating sides. Pull the ends of the braid to the back with a #18 chenille needle.

    Trim all the threads on the back to ¾" and flatten out the ends. These can be stitched loosely in place with silk sewing thread to keep them behind the embroidered areas.

    Cut the backing fabric on all four sides near the edge of the frame, to keep as much behind the ground fabric as possible. The picture can be mounted on a board as is, or can have a layer of acid-free tissue paper behind it for protection.

// = Stitch Direction

Basket of Fruit

ELSA T. COSE

Photo by David Feisner.

See Color Plate 15.

Overall Size: 5½" x 6".

MATERIALS

    10 yards #10 Japanese gold
    10 yards antique gold lamé or twist
    3 yards medium gold crinkle
    3 yards very fine gold crinkle
    ⅓ yard antique gold cord
    One skein silk floss in each of the following colors: red, orange, yellow-green,
    light green, medium green, dark green, brown
    One spool gold silk sewing thread
    One package #10 crewel needles
    #18 chenille needle
    #20 chenille needle
    3" x 5" piece of gray felt
    3" x 5" piece of gold felt
    14" x 16" piece of linen or muslin for backing
    15" x 15" piece of ground fabric
    Stretcher frame

PREPARATION

    A. Stretch the backing fabric on the frame.
    B. Attach the ground fabric to the backing.

C. Trace the design onto the fabric, using dressmaker's carbon.

D. Go over all traced lines with stitching. Use waxed silk sewing thread in running stitch on the basket, orange, and pear. Use a single strand of red floss in split stitch around each grape, medium green floss around each leaf.

Color Key (for leaves)
L: Light green floss
M: Medium green floss
D: Dark green floss

DIRECTIONS

1. Pad all the grapes except the three smallest ones with a layer of gray felt. Cut the felt smaller than actual size, so that when laid in place the red split stitch will show around it. Stitch felt in place.

2. Use a single strand of red silk floss for satin stitch on all the grapes. Take the first stitch across the center, covering the felt and split stitch. Work from the center to one side, then from the center to the other side, with all stitches parallel to the center stitch. The stitch direction of each grape is indicated on the pattern by double lines. Fill in the little areas between the grapes with satin stitch in a horizontal direction. A very fine line can be left between all the grapes, to allow room for a metal thread to be used around each later.

3. Use a single strand of green floss in long and short stitch for the leaves. The shades of green are indicated in the Color Key; the stitch direction is shown with the design sketch. Do the outer edge of the leaf first, making the first stitch at the tip of the leaf, and working one side. Then work from the tip down the other side. All stitches will come up near but not at the center vein. Shade with contrasting green by coming up through the first row and going down on the vein line. Stagger the lengths of these stitches. Do all the leaves in same manner. The leaf with the turned-up edge has satin stitch on its underside. Use the darkest shade of green for a line of split stitch in each center vein.

4. Pad the orange with two layers of gold felt, having the first layer only 1" across. Stitch the second layer on top, almost full size. Use a Flair pen to mark the dot of the navel on the felt. Open out the #10 gold and fold in half. Anchor the fold over the dot with a few stitches of orange silk floss, pulling rather tightly to dimple the felt. Curl the two strands of gold around the starting point in a clockwise direction, couching over both strands with the orange floss and almost completely covering the gold. After one complete round, start spacing the stitches a little apart. When the circle is large enough to reach the edge of the orange, cut the gold, leaving 1-inch tails, and pull the tails to the back with a #18 chenille needle. Start a new row at upper right of the orange, and lay alongside the circle, continuing to brick the stitches. Cut and sink at upper left. Continue with additional rows in this manner until the orange is complete. It may be necessary to add couching stitches if spaces get too large.

5. The pear is done in Italian shading. Do the outer row first, starting at the bottom right. Couch two strands of #10 gold with a single strand of yellow-green floss, making the stitches so close together that the gold is almost completely covered, but spacing the stitches irregularly. Sink the end of the row at lower left. Start the second row on lower right, keeping the stitches at irregular intervals; do not brick. Space the stitches farther apart on upper right to allow light to reflect off the gold. Fill the area by starting all the rows at lower right. Every few rows, put in a short row, to give added dimension. As the pear gradually fills in, the couching stitches are getting farther apart. When the stitches are more than ⅛" apart, then brick. A few stitches of brown floss can be used for the navel.

6. The basket is two strands of lamé or twist couched together in straight horizontal lines, with the ends pulled through to the back at the beginning and end of each row. Lay the first row across the middle, on traced line, couching in place with brown floss only where the gold crosses vertical lines. Couch three stitches together to make a heavy line, and three stitches on the right and left edges. Work parallel rows from the center down to the bottom, and then from the center up to the top.

7. Lay two rows of antique gold cord at the bottom of the basket, sinking the cord at either side with a #18 chenille needle.

8. Lay a single strand of medium-size gold crinkle around the outer edge of each leaf, couching in place with waxed silk sewing thread. Lay very fine crinkle around each grape in same manner.

9. Make the stems in brown satin stitch, and the tendrils with #10 gold couched closely with brown floss.

Trim all the threads on the back to ¾ ", and flatten out the ends. These can be stitched loosely in place with silk sewing thread to keep them behind the embroidered areas.

Cut the backing fabric on all four sides near the edge of the frame, to keep as much behind the ground fabric as possible. The picture can be mounted on a board as is, or can have a layer of acid-free tissue paper behind it for protection.

Plate 1. Little Town at Dusk *Betty Bohannon* Photo: *John Ogden Studios*

Plate 2. Pattern Intoxication *Marion Scoular* Photo: *Charles W. Haralson*

Plate 3. Pulled Thread and Assisi Embroidery *Jane W. Zimmerman*
Photo: Jane W. Zimmerman

Plate 4. Pulled Thread and Florentine Embroidery *Jane W. Zimmerman*
Photo: Jane W. Zimmerman

Plate 5. Squirrel on Branch *Audrey Francini* Photo: Loy Westbury

Plate 6. Floral *Audrey Francini* Photo: Loy Westbury

Plate 7. Bouquet *Audrey Francini* Photo: Loy Westbury

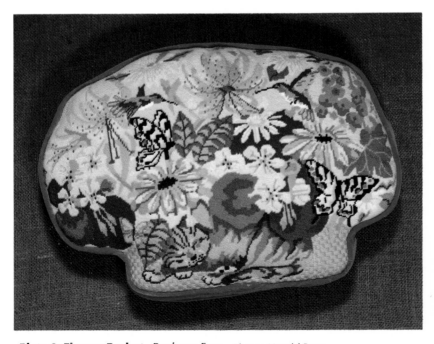

Plate 8. Flower Basket *Barbara Eyre* Photo: Harold Pratt

Plate 9. Squirrel *Barbara Eyre* Photo: Harold Pratt

Plate 10. Christmas Wreath *Barbara Eyre* Photo: Harold Pratt

Plate 11. Court Lady with Mirror *Mary Ascot*
Photo: Bob Talley

Plate 12. Horses' Heads *Gay Ann Rogers* *Photo: Gay Ann Rogers*

Plate 13. Pottery *Gay Ann Rogers* *Photo: Gay Ann Rogers*

Plate 14. Bird of Paradise *Elsa T. Cose* *Photo: Patricia Lambert*

Plate 15. Basket of Fruit *Elsa T. Cose* Photo: Patricia Lambert

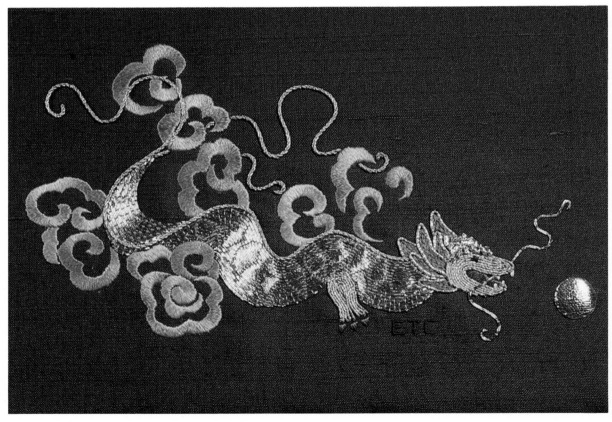

Plate 16. Happy Dragon *Elsa T. Cose* Photo: Patricia Lambert

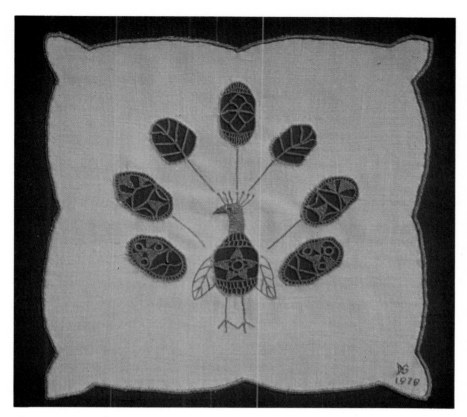

Plate 17. Peacock on Linen *Dorrit Gutterson* Photo: *Helen Wilson Sherman*

Plate 18. Peacock on Canvas *Dorrit Gutterson* Photo: *Helen Wilson Sherman*

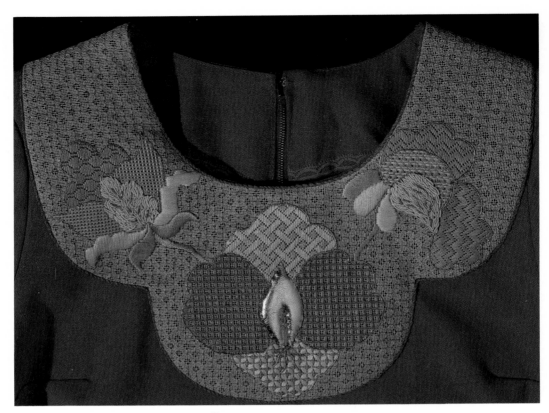

Plate 19. Caftan Yoke *Posy McMillen*   Photo: Lee Angle Photography Ltd.

Plate 20. Ocean Floor *Linda Labis Collette*   Photo: Armen Tachjian

Plate 21. Chestnut Branch *Catherine Staneslow*
Photo: Al Le Claire

Plate 22. Skunk Cabbage *Catherine Staneslow*
Photo: Al Le Claire

Plate 23. Balloon Race *Catherine Staneslow* *Photo: Al Le Claire*

Plate 24. Peaceable Kingdom *Doris Thacher* *Photo: Jan Thacher*

Plate 25. Fraktur *Doris Thacher* Photo: Jan Thacher

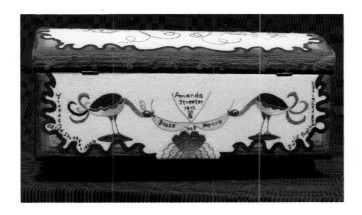

Plate 26. Deed Box *Doris Thacher* Photo: Jan Thacher

Plate 27. Alleluia *Minna Sturke* Photo: Henry Rorden

Plate 28. Little Fisherman *Judith Savage Becker* Photo: Don Servais

Plate 29. Diamond *Shay Pendray* Photo: *Jack Kausch*

Plate 30. Medallion *Shay Pendray* Photo: *Jack Kausch*

Plate 31. If God Be the Guide *Ginnie Thompson*
Photo: McKenzie Dickerson

Plate 32. Glory Be to God for Dappled Things
Ginnie Thompson   *Photo: McKenzie Dickerson*

// = Stitch Direction

Happy Dragon

ELSA T. COSE

See Color Plate 16.

Photo by David Feisner.

Overall Size: 7½" long x 4" high.

MATERIALS

One skein #5 Japanese gold
1 yard gold cord, heavy
1 yard gold twist, fine
1 yard silver twist, fine
1 sq. inch silver kid
1 sq. inch felt
3 inches silver check purl, medium
One spool gold silk sewing thread
One spool gray silk sewing thread
One skein medium aqua silk floss
One skein dark aqua silk floss
One skein pink silk floss

One skein purple silk floss
One skein golden-brown silk floss
One strand white silk floss
One strand black silk floss
One package #10 crewel needles
#18 chenille needle
#20 chenille needle
12" x 12" piece of linen or muslin for backing
12" x 12" piece of ground fabric
Stretcher frame
Index card

PREPARATION

    A. Stretch the backing fabric on the frame.

    B. Attach the ground fabric to the backing.

    C. Trace the design onto the fabric with dressmaker's carbon.

    D. Go over all traced lines with stitching. Use a single strand of silk floss around each cloud in appropriate color, in split stitch. Go over all other lines in running stitch with silk sewing thread.

DIRECTIONS

    1. All the clouds are in slanted satin stitch. Use Color Plate 16 as a guide for color placement.

    2. Lay two strands of fine silver twist couched with gold silk sewing thread on the leg and face, with the first row along the outer edge. Add enough rows to fill in area.

    3. Use brown silk floss, a single strand in a #10 crewel needle, to make the claws and the tongue. A few stitches of white floss can make the fangs; a few stitches of black can be placed right on top of the twist to make the eye. The whiskers are each two strands of Japanese gold laid together and couched with gold silk sewing thread. (When pulling the gold through to the back of the fabric, taper the sinking so that the ends of the whiskers will curl more easily.) Lay a strand of silver twist over the traced lines of the mane, couching with gray silk sewing thread. Fill in each area of the mane with split stitch, using two strands of the dark aqua floss. Cut the silver check purl into small pieces and sew into place with gray silk sewing thread on the top of the head.

    4. Lay a strand of heavy gold cord along the spine, sinking the end at the head, and laying along the traced line, sewing into place with silk sewing thread. At the tail, continue right over the satin-stitch clouds, and sink at the very end. Lay two more pieces, but sink these before and after the clouds, to make them appear underneath.

    5. Cut ten pieces of index card to fit into scales on the body. Sew into place with silk sewing thread, using only four stitches, one on each side. Beginning at the mane, lay two strands of Japanese gold alongside the cord, couching with one strand of dark aqua floss. Couching stitches will be taken only before the piece of card, and again on the other side of the card; this will define the scales. The row will continue all the way along the gold cord and will be sunk when the cloud is reached. Each subsequent row of Japanese gold will begin at the head, and will be laid alongside the last row, with the row ending near the tail. (If additional stitches are needed to hold the gold more firmly, use gold silk sewing thread.) Short rows of gold may be needed to round out the belly (see design sketch).

6. The turned-up part of the tail is filled with rows of Japanese gold, couched with dark aqua floss in a bricking pattern. Lay the first row of two strands along the uppermost edge, sinking the strands at the beginning and end of each row. Add enough rows to fill the area.

7. For the pearl, cut a piece of felt slightly smaller than the traced size, and sew into place with stitches around the outer edge only. Cut a piece of silver kid slightly larger than the circle, and sew into place with gray silk sewing thread. Sew by bringing the needle up through the leather at a slant, so that the silver coating is not pierced, and take the needle down through the fabric only.

Trim all the threads on the back to ¾", and flatten out the ends. These can be stitched loosely in place with silk sewing thread to keep them behind the embroidered areas.

Cut the backing fabric on all four sides near the edge of the frame, to keep as much behind the ground fabric as possible. Picture can be mounted on a board as is, or can have a layer of acid-free tissue paper behind it for protection.

Peacock
Hedebo on Linen

DORRIT GUTTERSON

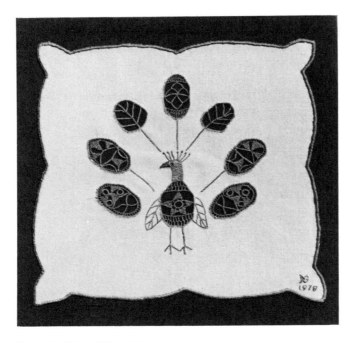

Photo by Helen Wilson Sherman.

See Color Plate 17.

Overall Size: 7½″ x 6¾″.

MATERIALS
White linen
#12 D.M.C. perle cotton—brown

Stitch Key
Seven feathers and bird's body: Hedebo
A: Chain stitch
B: Outline stitch
C: French knots
D: Closed herringbone stitch

DIRECTIONS

To make the hedebo buttonhole stitch, insert needle into the back of the work and leave a small loop. Insert needle again through the back of the loop and pull tight.

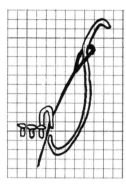

To make a pyramid of hedebo buttonhole stitches, work the required amount of hedebo buttonhole from left to right. Overcast the back. Succeeding hedebo buttonhole rows have one stitch less at either end of the row. Repeat until all stitches have been decreased to form a pyramid.

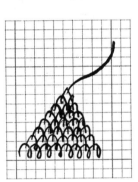

Design sketches for Peacock: Hedebo on Linen follow, on pages 96 and 97.

Peacock:
Hedebo
on Linen

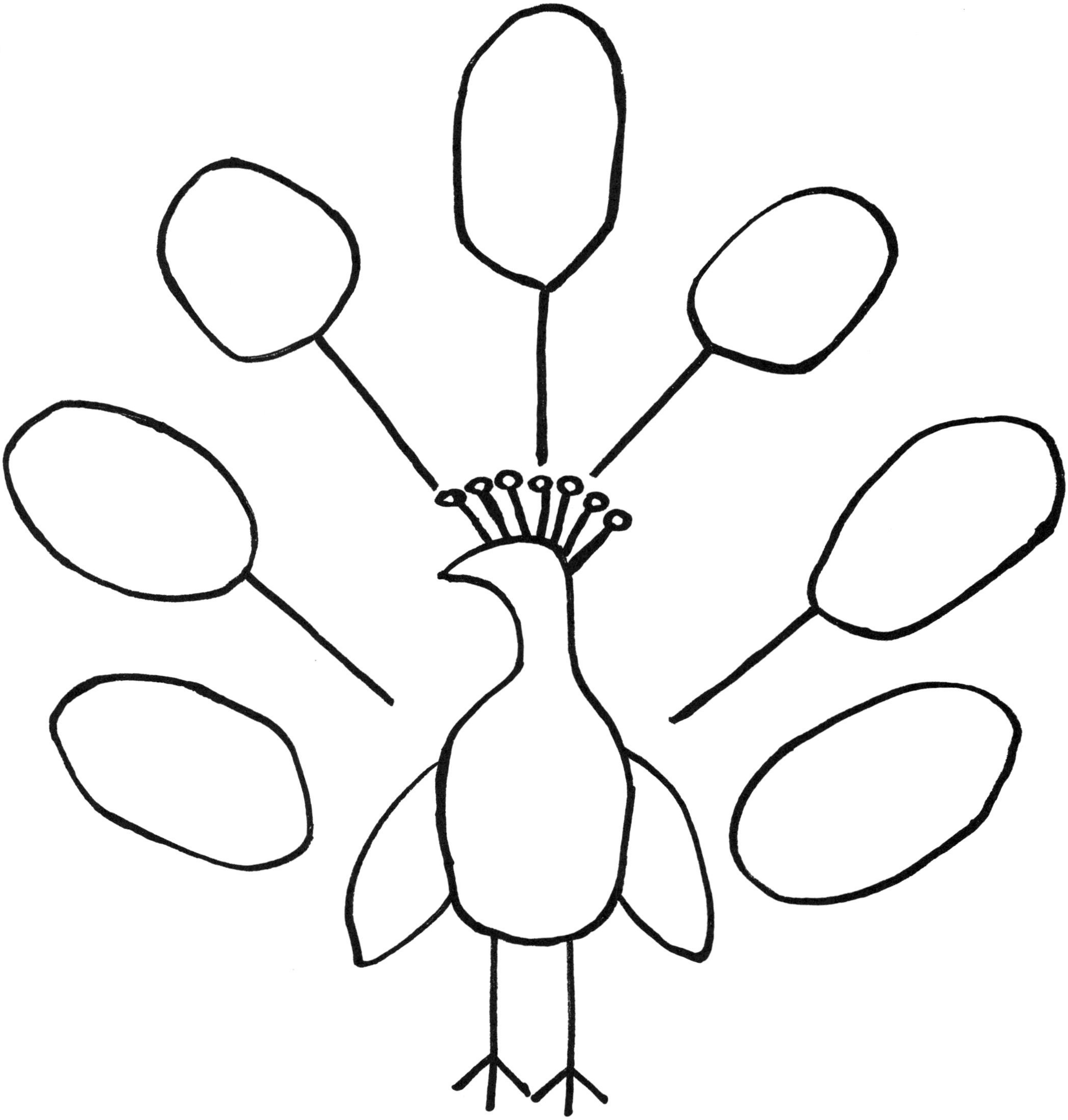

Peacock:
Hedebo
on Linen

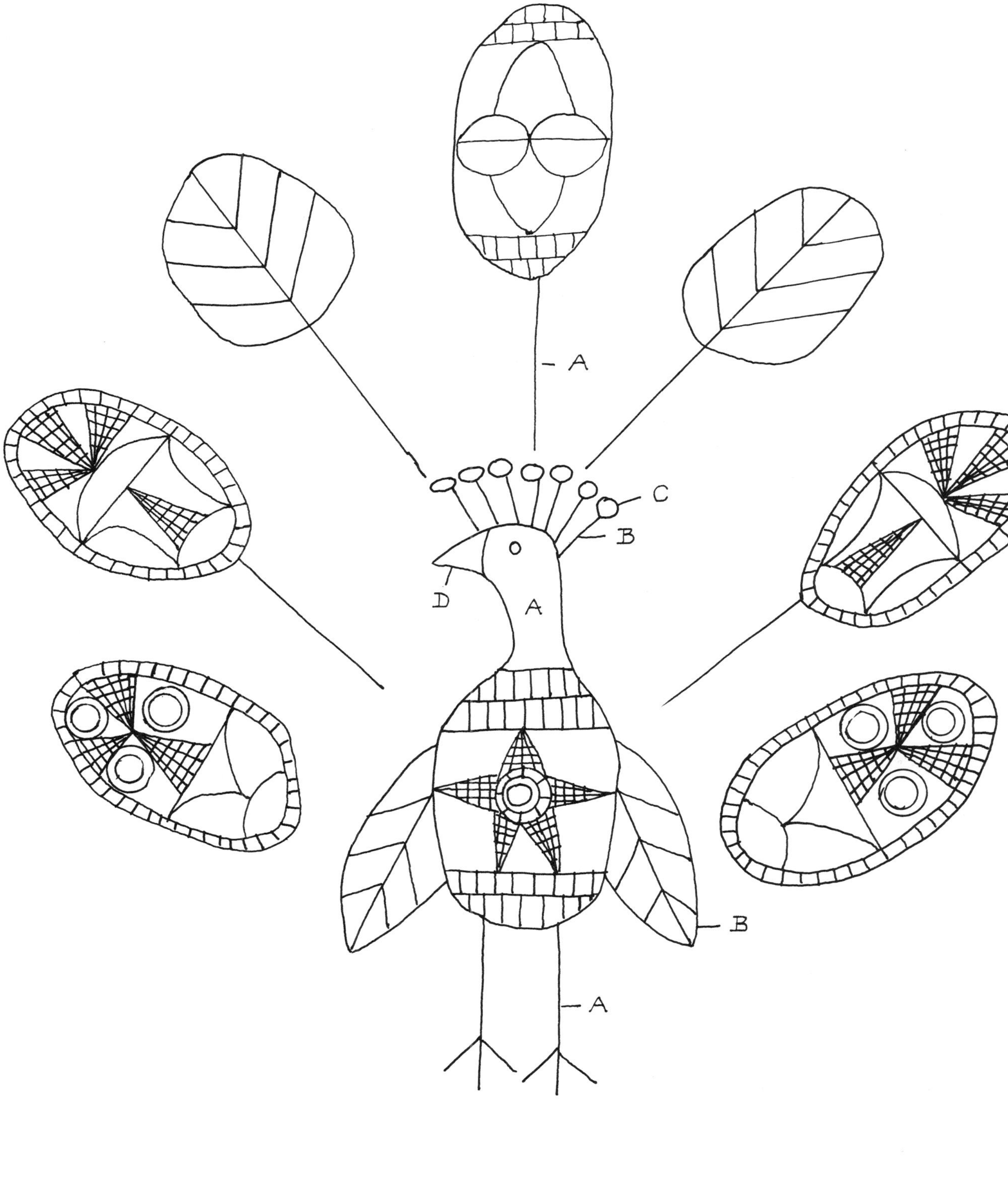

Peacock
Hedebo on Canvas

DORRIT GUTTERSON

Photo by Helen Wilson Sherman.

See Color Plate 18.

Overall Size: 7½" x 7¼".

MATERIALS (with letter/color key)
#14 interlocking canvas
#8 perle cotton—blue (B)
#8 perle cotton—green (G)
#5 perle cotton—gold (Go)

Stitch Key
Seven feathers and bird's body: Hedebo
Bird's head: Encroaching Gobelin stitch
Top of bird's head: Elongated French knots
Beak: Closed herringbone stitch
Wings: Open fly stitch
Straight lines and bird's legs: Whipped backstitch

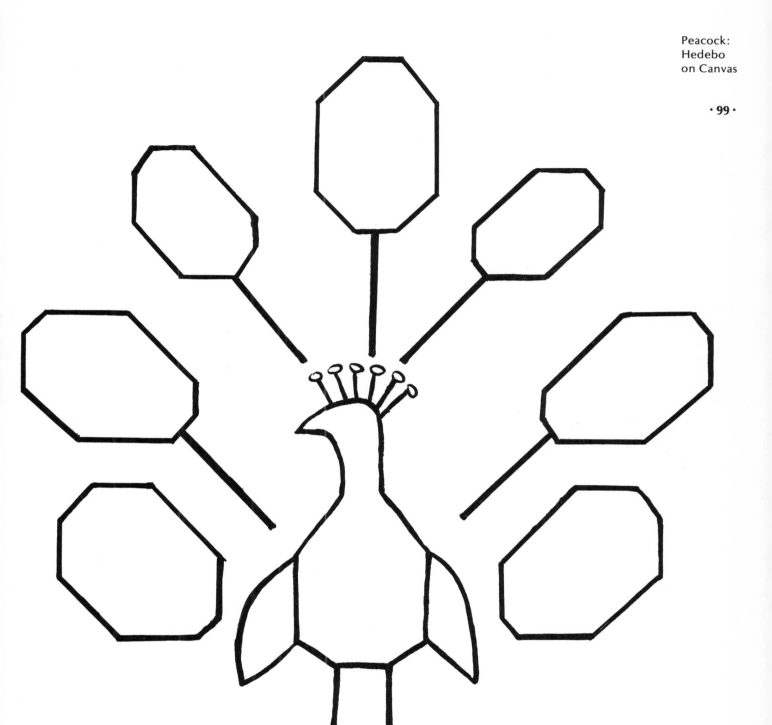

Peacock:
Hedebo
on Canvas

· 100 ·

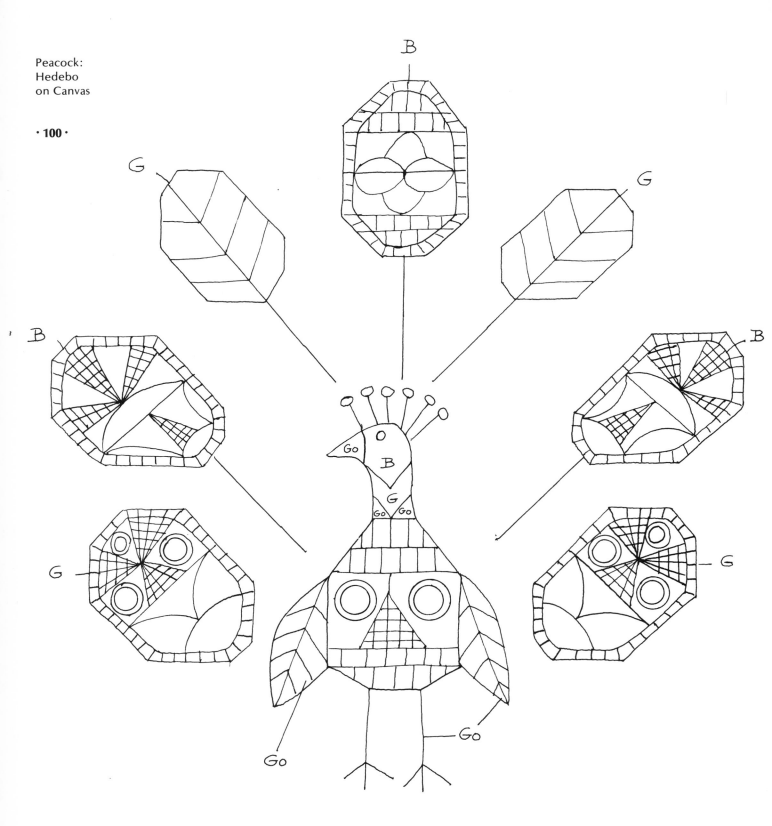

Caftan Yoke

POSY McMILLEN

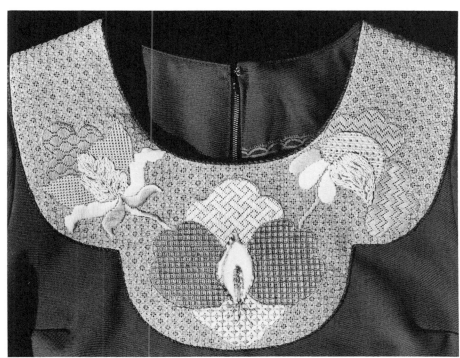

See Color Plate 19.

Photo by Lee Angle Photography Ltd.

Overall Size: Your size.

MATERIALS (with letter/color key)

16" x 16" stretcher frame
16" x 16" piece 24-mesh gray congress cloth
Tapestry #22 and chenille #22 or #24 needles
6" x 6" piece white felt
Gray floss (Gr)
#8 Japanese gold
#8 bright purl check
Fine gold metallic floss thread (GM)
3" x 3" piece gold kid (GK)
Gold cordonnet (GC)

Au Ver à Soie French silks:
    light yellow-green (LYG)
    medium yellow-green (MYG)
    aqua (A)
    rose (R)
    pink (P)
    gray-green (GrG)
Zwicky Swiss silks:
    light pink (LPS)
    medium pink (MPS)

DIRECTIONS

1. Draw the design on the canvas.
2. Do pulled satin stitches.
3. Do laid work (see diagrams, pages 105 and 106) with silk and metal threads.
4. Do the bullion knots.
5. Do triple leviathan and ribbon filling (see graph diagram, page 106).
6. Pad the leaves with one layer of felt, using a sewing needle (see paddings diagrams, page 107).
7. Satin-stitch over the felt, using 4-ply French silk.
8. Pad the center of the middle flowers with two layers of felt. Baste each layer—smaller one first—separately. Using a fine metallic thread, baste the piece of gold kid on in the same manner as the felt.
9. With four strands of rose silk, make long French knots in the voided area of the gold kid.
10. Using the fine metallic thread, couch all the outlines of the flowers with one strand of #8 Japanese gold.
11. Cut #8 bright purl check in ¼-inch pieces and sew in scattered places on top of the bullion knots.
12. Do background in Greek cross filling, using 2-ply gray floss.

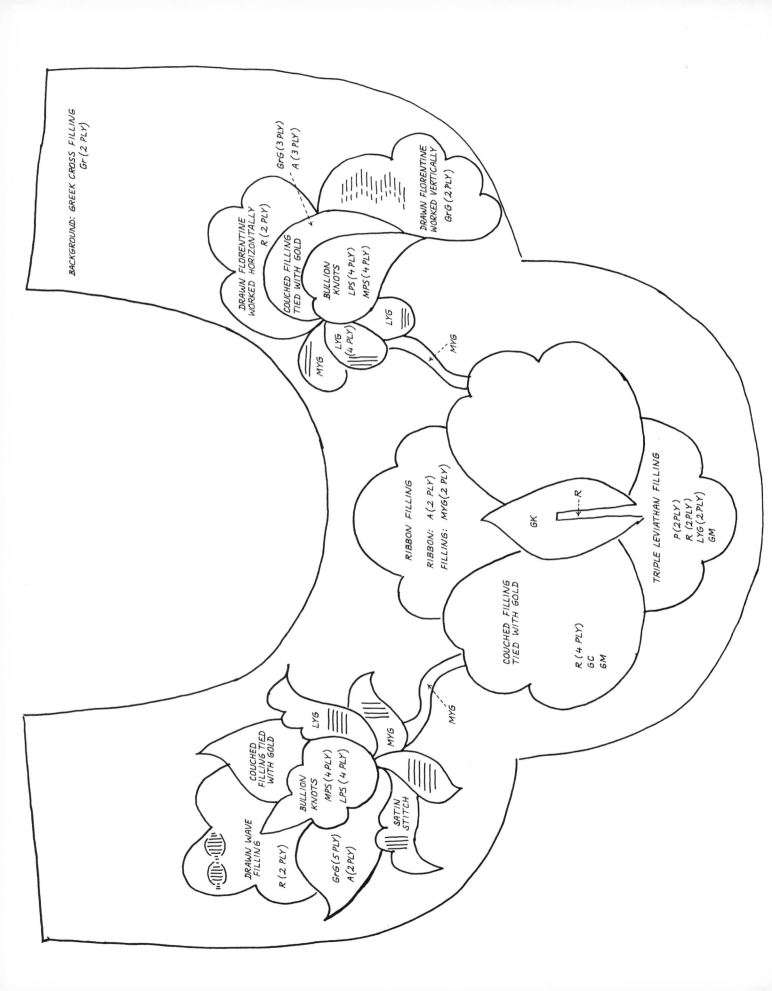

LAID WORK
ROWS
Green (5 ply), vertical
Aqua (2 ply), horizontal
Gold metallic, X's

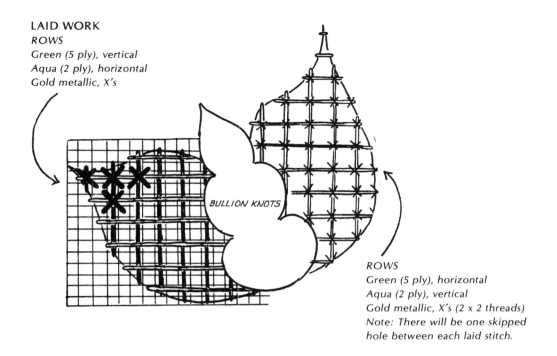

BULLION KNOTS

ROWS
Green (5 ply), horizontal
Aqua (2 ply), vertical
Gold metallic, X's (2 x 2 threads)
*Note: There will be one skipped
hole between each laid stitch.*

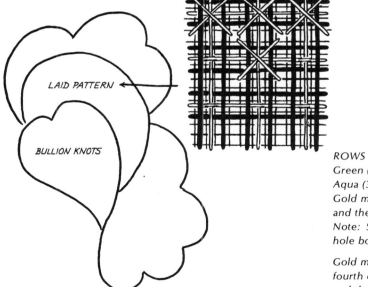

LAID PATTERN

BULLION KNOTS

ROWS
Green (3 ply), vertical
Aqua (3 ply), horizontal
*Gold metallic, vertical, horizontal,
and then X's (4 x 4 threads)*
*Note: Silk will be laid every other
hole both vertically and horizontally.*

*Gold metallic will be laid every
fourth canvas hole both directions
and then tied down with large X's.*

Caftan Yoke

LAID WORK
ROWS
Rose (4 ply), vertical, every fourth canvas hole
Rose (4 ply), horizontal, every fourth canvas hole
Gold cordonnet, vertical, in each consecutive hole to right of silk
Gold cordonnet, horizontal, in each consecutive hole below silk
Gold metallic, X's, to tie down silk
and cordonnet (3 x 3 threads)

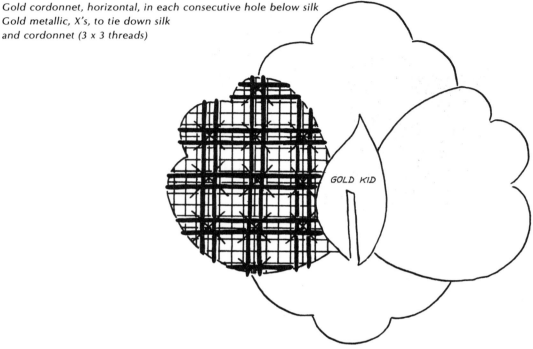

GOLD KID

RIBBON FILLING
Do all ribbons in 2-ply aqua first.
Then fill in spaces with 2-ply medium yellow-green.

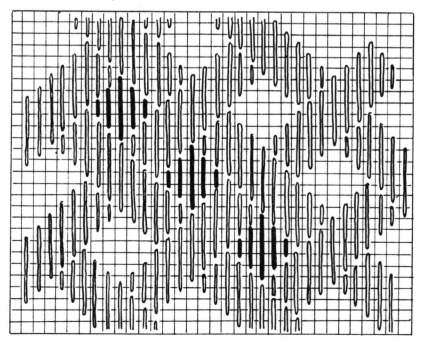

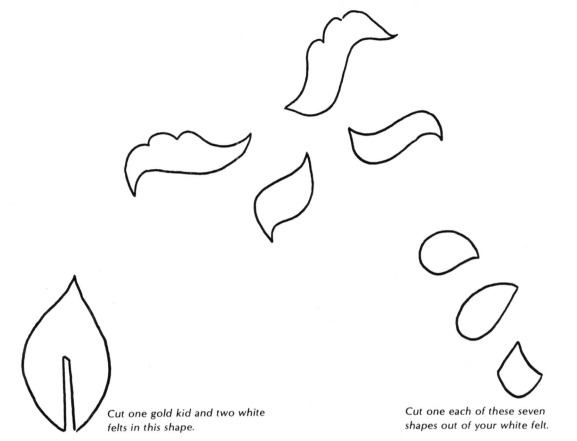

Cut one gold kid and two white felts in this shape.

Cut one each of these seven shapes out of your white felt.

Ocean Floor

LINDA LABIS COLLETTE

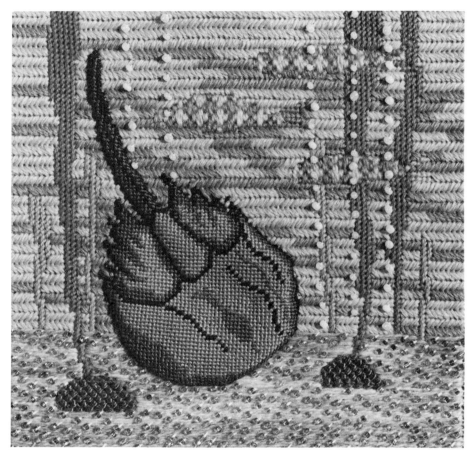

Photo by Armen Tachjian.

See Color
Plate 20.

Overall Size: 8″ x 8″.

MATERIALS

18-mesh mono canvas
22-mesh mono canvas for appliqué
6-strand floss
Perle cotton
Crewel wool

Stitch, Color, and Thread Key
A: Upright cross-stitch, medium brown, perle cotton
B: Encroaching Gobelin stitch, light and medium dark yellow-green, 6-strand floss
C: Hungarian stitch, light and medium light brick, crewel wool
D: Reverse tent stitch (Kalem), two lightest shades aqua-green, crewel wool
E: Roumanian couching stitch, light sand color, crewel wool
F: Tent stitch, two medium shades rust, 6-strand floss

The crab, F, is an appliqué. Place the crab in the middle of a 7-inch square of 22-mesh canvas. After working it, outline it in tent stitch in dark brown. Appliqué it to the background of Ocean Floor, giving dimension to the piece. If desired, you may pad the crab to give even more dimension.

Bubbles may be appliquéd here and there by using small, iridescent pearl beads. Beads may also be sewn at random on the ocean floor (see Color Plate 20).

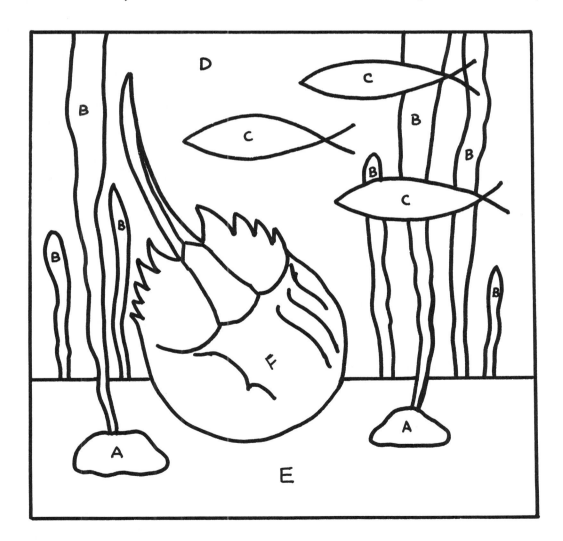

Chestnut Branch

CATHERINE STANESLOW

Photo by Al LeClaire.

See Color Plate 21.

Overall Size: 16" x 8".

MATERIALS

#18 mono canvas, 20" x 12" (for background)
#24 mono canvas, three pieces, each 7" x 8" (for burrs)
Lightest shade olive green Persian yarn (for background)
Three lower shades olive green Persian yarn (for leaves)
Gray Persian yarn (for branch)
Three shades brown mouline (for burrs of top and bottom borders)
One medium-shade gold mouline (for leaves of top and bottom borders)
One light beige mouline (for background of top and bottom borders)
Two shades ecru mouline (for border around complete piece)
Metal thread, if desired (for couching with medium shade in burrs in borders and for branch couching)

Stitch Key

Borders, leaves, and chestnuts on branch: Tent stitch
Outside border all around: Florentine stitch
Background of branch: Mosaic stitch
Branch: Couching and metal threads

DIRECTIONS

1. Lay in the branch first, using several threads of gray yarn twisted together and tapering as the branch gets smaller. Couch this down in place.

2. Work the leaves and three small burrs in tent stitch. Make the nuts prickly by taking short stitches at random over the tent stitches after the background has been worked.

3. The background of the branch is worked in the lightest shade of olive green in diagonal mosaic stitch.

4. The borders top and bottom are worked in tent stitch. The round burrs are shaded in three shades of brown. The leaves are worked flat in gold. The background is a light beige.

5. The strips of metallic gold on each side are laid in and couched down with the medium shade of the brown used in the top and bottom borders.

6. The border around the entire piece is worked in straight stitches in two shades of ecru as shown in the graph on page 114. The small diamonds are in a darker shade of ecru.

7. Using the #24 mono canvas, work a chestnut burr in the center of each square. For shading of the burrs, use the plan below. After they have been appliquéd to the main piece, work the nut ready to drop from the burr on the left. This is done in satin stitch with the lightest shade of the brown mouline used in bottom border.

A design sketch for Chestnut Branch, a plan for its dimensions part by part, and instructions for shading the chestnuts and for embroidering the border of the design follow, on pages 112 through 114.

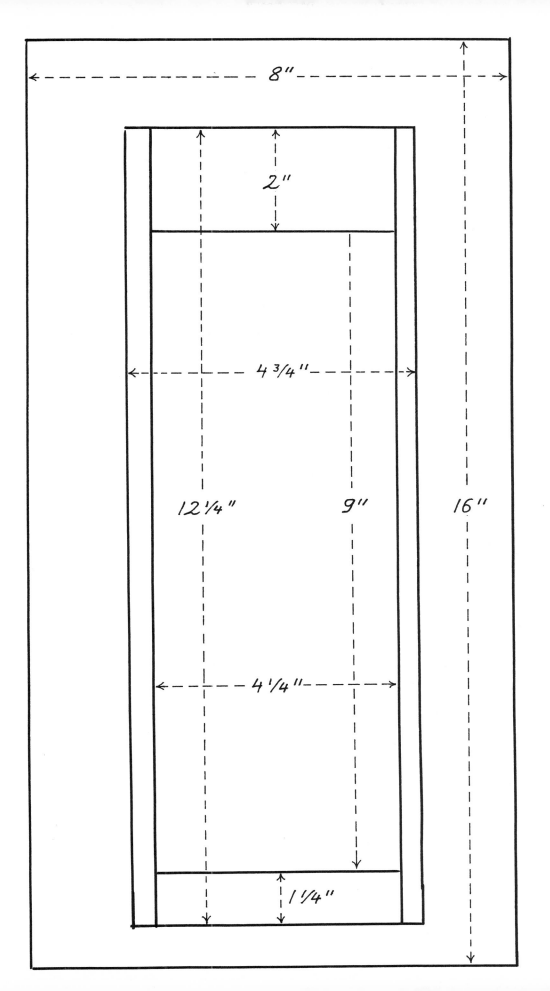

8"

2"

4 3/4"

12 1/4"   9"   16"

4 1/4"

1 1/4"

Chestnut
Branch

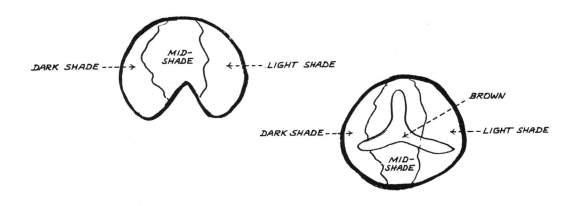

Shading Plan for Chestnuts

Border of Chestnut Panel

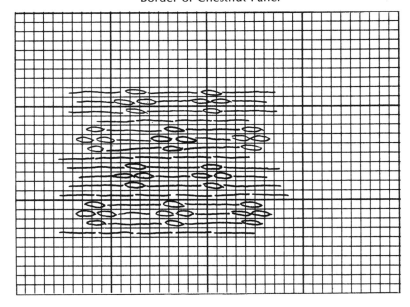

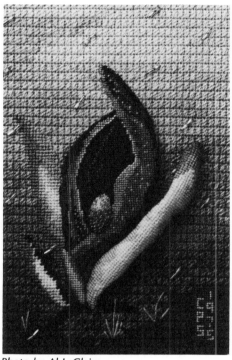

Photo by Al LeClaire.

Skunk Cabbage in the Rain

CATHERINE STANESLOW

See Color Plate 22.

Overall Size: 9" x 6¼".

MATERIALS

#14 mono canvas, 14" x 11" (for the main piece)
#18 mono canvas, 9" x 12" (for sepals, or hood)
#18 mono canvas, about 8" x 8" (for large leaf)
#24 mono canvas, 6" x 6" (for spadix, or small oval)
Three or four shades olive drab Persian yarn (for background)
Several shades yellow-green Persian yarn (for leaves)
Wine-red and rose shades and brown mouline (for sepals)
Gold shades mouline (for spadix)
About three dozen gold seed beads
About three dozen silver bugle beads

Stitch Key
Design: Tent stitch
Background: Cashmere stitch

DIRECTIONS

1. On #14 mono canvas, trace the outline of the skunk cabbage and its leaves. Omit the lines for the grasses and the rain. (These are put in freehand after all the other work is done.) On #18 mono, mark all the lines for the sepals, or hood, in the center of your canvas. On the other piece of #18 mono (the 8-inch square), mark off the big leaf. Lastly, on the #24 mono, mark off the spadix (the small oval shape) in the center of the canvas.

2. Work the spadix in tent stitch in three shades of gold. Now the piece is ready to bead. Using a bead needle or a very fine sewing needle and sewing thread, sew the gold seed beads to the worked canvas. Bead heavily near the bottom and sparingly near the top.

3. Work the sepals or hood, also in tent stitch. Before starting, make sure you have marked the oval shape where the spadix fits. It should be slightly smaller than the piece just worked, so that when the spadix is appliquéd to the sepals, it can be padded. The sepals are shaded as marked in the design sketch. In shading the sepals—which form a hood over the spadix—think of their cupped shape.

4. Put these two completed pieces together. Ravel out all the edges of the spadix piece right up to the tent stitches. Into the needle, thread the top-center thread of canvas and pull it through the top center of the place left for it in the sepal piece. Repeat this in the center bottom and center of each side. When your pieces line up with each other, start working each canvas thread through the work to the back. When three-quarters of the way around, tuck a few scraps of wool inside to pad it slightly.

5. Work the large leaf in shades of yellow-green wool as shown in diagram sketch.

6. On the main piece, work the other two leaves, adding brown as shown in the sketch.

7. Work the background, but first check to make sure the sepals are lined up. The large leaf will seem too wide as this is folded when it is appliquéd. The background, in cashmere stitch, is shaded from light at the top to dark at the bottom.

8. When all the background has been completed, appliqué the sepal piece in place. Next, fold the large leaf down the middle vertically and fit the left side tightly against the sepal, as shown. It curves on a slight diagonal.

9. Last, do the small clumps of grass in a medium yellow-green wool. Using a single thread, lay in long stitches as desired. The rain is made by putting two bugle beads end-to-end in the areas shown in the line drawing.

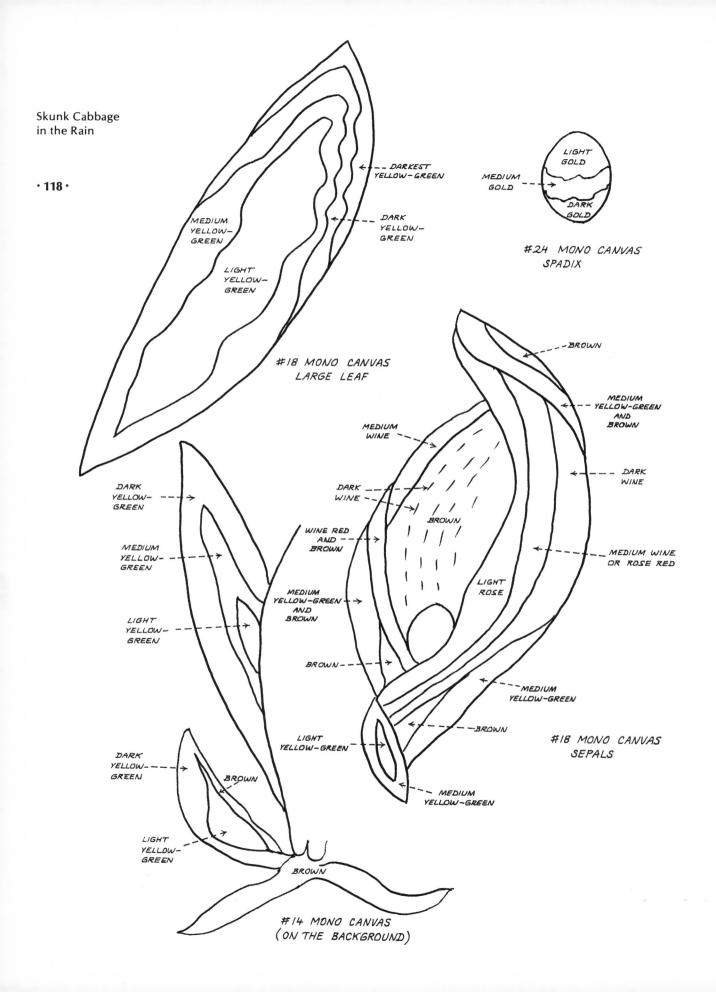

DARKEST
YELLOW-GREEN

DARK
YELLOW-
GREEN

MEDIUM
YELLOW-
GREEN

LIGHT
YELLOW-
GREEN

#18 MONO CANVAS
LARGE LEAF

LIGHT
GOLD

MEDIUM
GOLD

DARK
GOLD

#24 MONO CANVAS
SPADIX

BROWN

MEDIUM
YELLOW-GREEN
AND
BROWN

DARK
WINE

MEDIUM WINE
OR ROSE RED

MEDIUM
WINE

DARK
WINE

BROWN

WINE RED
AND
BROWN

LIGHT
ROSE

DARK
YELLOW-
GREEN

MEDIUM
YELLOW-
GREEN

MEDIUM
YELLOW-GREEN
AND
BROWN

LIGHT
YELLOW-
GREEN

BROWN

MEDIUM
YELLOW-GREEN

BROWN

LIGHT
YELLOW-GREEN

#18 MONO CANVAS
SEPALS

MEDIUM
YELLOW-GREEN

DARK
YELLOW-
GREEN

BROWN

LIGHT
YELLOW-
GREEN

BROWN

#14 MONO CANVAS
(ON THE BACKGROUND)

Balloon Race

CATHERINE STANESLOW

Photo by Al LeClaire.

*See Color
Plate 23.*

Overall Size: 10″ x 14″.

MATERIALS

#14 mono canvas, 14″ x 18″ (for background piece)
#18 mono canvas, 10″ x 10½″ (for largest balloon)
#24 mono canvas, 8¼″ x 8¾″ (for medium-sized balloon)
Three shades gray Persian or crewel yarn (for sky)
Two shades lavender and one dark blue Persian or crewel yarn (for distant mountains)
Two shades tan and two shades blue-green Persian or crewel yarn (for fields)
Three shades olive green Persian or crewel yarn (for trees)
Three shades several colors mouline or French tapestry silk (for balloons)

Stitch Key

Sky, mountains, and balloons: Tent stitch
Fields: Slanted Gobelin stitch
Trees and hedgerows: French knots

DIRECTIONS

1. Draw the design any size, using as many balloons as desired; sizes for the original balloons are, however, given opposite, on page 121.

2. Plan the balloon patterns and color schemes. The two largest ones are worked on smaller-mesh canvas and appliquéd to the main piece. But this is not necessary; they may be worked directly on the canvas.

3. If appliqué is planned, work the two pieces separately. Work the background and then appliqué the balloons to it.

4. The sky and mountains are all worked in tent stitch as shown in the design sketch.

5. Work the fields in slanted encroaching Gobelin over two threads. Vary the colors of the fields, using two shades of tan and two shades of blue-green, as you may wish.

6. Work the hedgerows between the fields with dark and medium olive green. Shade the trees with three shades of olive green.

7. Work the balloons, using three shades of each color. Keep the light source constant in the entire design.

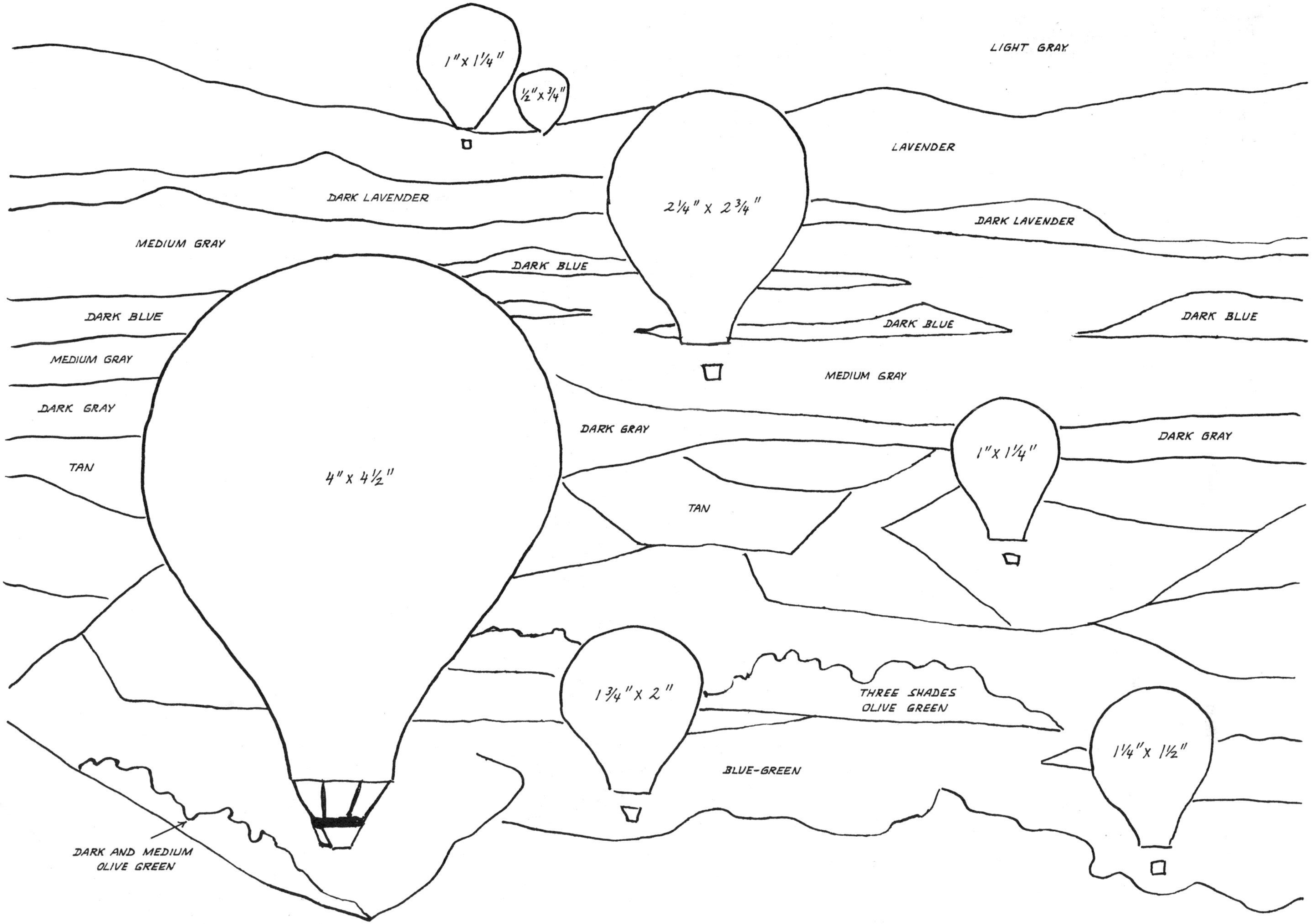

1" x 1¼"
½" x ¾"
LIGHT GRAY
LAVENDER
2¼" x 2¾"
DARK LAVENDER
DARK LAVENDER
MEDIUM GRAY
DARK BLUE
DARK BLUE
DARK BLUE
DARK BLUE
MEDIUM GRAY
MEDIUM GRAY
DARK GRAY
DARK GRAY
DARK GRAY
1" x 1¼"
TAN
4" x 4½"
TAN
1¾" x 2"
THREE SHADES
OLIVE GREEN
BLUE-GREEN
1¼" x 1½"
DARK AND MEDIUM
OLIVE GREEN

Peaceable Kingdom

DORIS THACHER

Photo by Jan Thacher.

*See Color
Plate 24.*

Overall Size: 26" x 20¾".

Stitch Key
B: Bullion knots
H: Herringbone stitch
O: Outline stitch
R: Roumanian stitch (variant; see page 133)
S: Satin stitch
T: Thacher stitch (see page 133)

Color Key

1:	Grass green	9:	Charcoal gray
2:	Blue-green	10:	Black
3:	Olive green	11:	Pink
4:	Marine blue	12:	Cream
5:	Sky blue	13:	Brown
6:	White	14:	Purple
7:	Red	15:	Orange-red
8:	Gold		

Color shades are a, b, c, d, and e; "a" is the lightest, "e" the darkest.

DIRECTIONS

The eyes of all the animals are done the same and are most important; they should be done first. The eye itself is done in white in satin stitches worked horizontally. The pupil is worked in black in satin stitch done vertically. The pupil should never touch the side of the eye itself.

Giraffe
Body: T-8b
Head: T-8a
Spots: T-8e
Mane: O-8e
Ears: T-8e
Tail: O-8e
Horns: O-13b, S-13b
Hooves: T-8e

Dragon
Head: T-15e
Snout: O-9e
Tongue: O-8c
"Fire": S-7b
Body: R-15e, R-15d, R-15c (at random). (Each scale is outlined in a different shade than it is worked in.)
Tail: R-15c, R-15d
Mane: R-15c, R-15d
Feet: R-15c

Mice (large and small)
Body: R-11a, R-11b, R-11c (lightest at top)
Head: R-11b
Ears: R-11c
Tail: O-11c

Skunk
Body: R-10, R-6, R-10
Head: R-10
Ears: R-10
Feet: R-10
Tail: R-10, R-6, R-10

Lamb
Body: B-6
Face: T-6

Lion
Body: T-8c, T-8d
Mane: T-8b, T-8c (at random),
O-8d
Face: T-8c (with touches of 8d)
Nose: T-9d
Chin: T-8a
Tail: T-8d
Pom-pom: O-8d

Snail
Body: R-11b
Head: R-11a
Tail: R-11c
Feelers: O-11c, S-11c

Goat
Haunches: T-9d
Stomach: T-9a, T-6
Head: T-9d
Horns: T-9d
Tail: T-9a, T-6
Ears: T-9b
Whiskers: O-9d

Ram
Body: B-6
Tail: B-9a
Horns: O-9b
Ears: O-9b

Leopard
Body: T-8d, T-8e, T-8a
Chest: T-8a
Face: T-8e
Tail: T-8e
Spots: S-13b
Ears: T-8a
Whiskers: O-13b
Pads: S-8b

Hummingbird
Upper wings: R-3a
Lower wings: R-3d
Upper body: R-3d
Lower body: R-7b
Head: R-3d
Tail: O-3d

Fish
Body: R-8b

Palm Tree and Grass Tufts
Trunk: R-3d, R-3c, R-3b, R-3a (work from
bottom up), R-3d, R-3c, R-3b, R-3a
Fronds: H-7d, H-7c
Grass tufts: R-3a, R-3b, R-3c, R-3d (at
random)

Grapes
Fruit: R-14a, R-14b
Leaves: R-3a
Veins in leaves: O-3d
Stems: O-3d

Flowers Below Mice
Petals: R-8a, R-8c
Centers: B-8d
Leaves: R-3a
Stems: O-3c

Flowers Around Skunk
Petals: R-8a
Outlines: O-7b
Leaves: R-8b
Stems: O-8b

Strawberries
Fruit: R-7a, R-7b
Dots in fruit: S-8b
Four small leaves: R-3b
Outer large leaves: R-3d
Inner large leaves: R-3c, R-3d, R-3c
Stems: O-3b

Flowers at Edge of Ocean
Petals: R-11b, R-11d, R-11c
Leaves: R-1b
Veins in leaves: O-1d
Stems: O-1a

Bush on Hill
Fronds: H-7a, H-7b, H-7c, H-7d

Mounds (ground and hill divisions)
Mound 1: T-1 (all five shades)
Mound 2: T-2 (all five shades)
Mound 3: T-3 (all five shades)
Mound 4: T-4 (all five shades)

All mounds are worked in Thacher stitch, running vertically and shaded from dark to light within each mound; be careful to blend shades, avoiding straight lines and sharp edges.

Ocean
Water: T-5 (shades a, b, c, and d—the lightest at the bottom—worked vertically)
Waves: T-6 (worked horizontally)
Dark wave: T-9a

MOUND 4

MOUND 3

MOUND 1

MOUND 2

Photo by Jan Thacher.

Fraktur

DORIS THACHER

See Color Plate 25.

Overall Size: 17″ x 17″.

Stitch Key
B: Bullion knots
C: Cross-stitch
H: Herringbone stitch
O: Outline stitch
R: Roumanian stitch (variant; see page 133)
S: Satin stitch

Color Key
1: Marine blue
2: White
3: Black
4: Grass green
5: Brown
6: Terra-cotta
7: Red

Color shades are a, b, c, and d; "a" is the lightest, "d" the darkest.

DIRECTIONS

To do the scalloped outside border, begin at the lower-left corner: R-1d, R-1c, R-1b, R-1d, R-1c, R-1b . . . Keep repeating this marine blue shading sequence around the entire border.

Large Leaf at Each of the Four Corners
Leaf markings: C-1d
Leaf fringe: H-1c
Outlines of leaf fringe: O-1d
Veins of leaf: O-1d
Stem: O-1d

Two Large Flowers at Top and at Bottom
Outer petals: R-1d, R-1c, R-1a, R-1d (shaded from outside in)
Inner petals: O-2
Center: B-2
Leaves: R-4c, R-4d
Stems: O-5
Budding flower: R-1a, R-1d

Six Small Flowers at Each Side
Petals: O-1d
Center: R-2
Leaves: R-4c
Stems: O-5

Center Frame
Entire frame: R-1d

Six Mounds
Top two mounds: R-4d
Middle two mounds: R-4c
Bottom two mounds: R-4b

Strawberries
Fruit: R-7b
Dots in fruit: S-2
Leaves: R-4d
Stem: O-5c

Left-hand Bird
Wings: R-5
Lower body: R-6
Head: R-5
Tail: R-5
Eye: S-3
Beak: S-3
Feet: O-3

Topmost Bird
Wings: R-1b
Lower body: R-6c
Head: R-5c
Tail: R-1b
Eye: S-3
Beak: S-3
Feet: O-3

Right-hand Bird
Wings: R-5c
Lower body: R-2
Head: R-5b
Tail: R-5b
Eye: S-3
Beak: S-3
Feet: O-3

Deer
Main body: O-6c, O-6d (shaded in)
Antlers: O-6d
Eye: S-3
Tail: B-6b
Feet: S-6d

Tree
Trunk: O-6b, O-6c, O-6d
Branches: O-6c
Leaves: R-4b, R-4c (at random), R-4d
Fruit: R-7b, R-7c (at random)

A design sketch for Fraktur follows, on page 130.

Photo by Jan Thacher.

Deed Box

DORIS THACHER

See Color Plate 26.

Overall Size: 12½″ x 14½″.

The embroiderer should see Color Plate 26 for the front and back of the deed box. The following design sketch is of the attractive end pieces for the box, with a scalloped border like that seen in the color plate.

Stitch Key
B: Buttonhole stitch
H: Herringbone stitch
O: Outline stitch
R: Roumanian stitch (variant; see page 133)
S: Satin stitch
T: Thacher stitch (see page 133)

Color Key
1: Marine blue
2: White
3: Brown
4: Grass Green
5: Gray
6: Pink
7: Red

Color shades are a, b, c, d, e, and f; "a" is the lightest, "f" the darkest.

DIRECTIONS

This design may be used as a pillow, a bag, a picture, or, with a little adapting, used three times as the sides and top of a box.

Queen Anne Scalloped Border

Outer Band: R-4e
Second band: R-4d
Third band: R-4c
First corner: R-4b
Second corner: R-4a
Third (inner) corner: R-4a
Scalloping: R-4f

Branch

R-1c, 1d, 1e, 1d, 1c—in this sequence starting at the lower edge

Leaves

Inner leaf: T-4c
Outer leaf: T-4a
Veins: O-4b
Stem: O-4b

Bird

Breast: T-6b, T-6c—these two working from top to bottom
Wing: T-4e
Scallop on wing and back: B-2
Back: O-4a (two rows), O-4d (two rows), O-4e (two rows)
Head: R-4d
Beak: S-3b
Eye: S-2
Pupil: S-3
Tail: H-6d (all five parts)
Shanks: T-6d
Legs: O-4d

Berries in Bird's Grip

Fruit: T-7b, T-7c, T-7d
Stems: O-4e

Strawberries

Fruit: T-7b, T-7c, T-7d (darkest at bottom)
Dots in fruit: S-4b
Leaves: R-4b, R-4c
Trefoil leaves: R-4c
Stems: O-4e (Don't complete these until you've done the background below; this way, they will lie on top.)

Background to Strawberries Section
Bottom band: R-1f
Second band: R-1e
Third and fourth bands: R-1d
Fifth and sixth bands: R-1e
Seventh and eighth bands: R-1f

Variant on Roumanian Stitch

Work from left to right. The yarn is always to the left of the needle.

1. Come up at A. Take a small stitch from B to C with the needle pointing down.

2. Take a small stitch from D to E with the needle pointing up.

3. Repeat. Keep stitches close together to cover fabric. The small stitches may vary in length but the exit points should never meet or overlap. The less linen threads you pick up with the needle (the smaller the stitch), the flatter the effect.

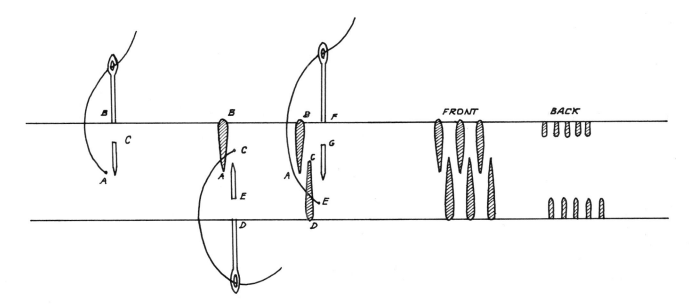

The Thacher Stitch

This stitch is comprised of rows of stem stitch. They vary in length and are used to fill large areas.

The thread is always on the left of the needle. When working *up* the needle points down, and when working *down* the needle points up.

When the end of a row is reached, a small extra stitch is taken alongside the last stitch before reversing the needle and starting on the next row.

Important: No two stitches should begin or end at the same place. Stitches are basically ½″ or less in length.

Photo by Photo Dynamics.

Alleluia

MINNA STURKE

See Color Plate 27.

Overall Size: Letters 3″ high; word 18″ across.

This pulpit fall is an example of ecclesiastical embroidery worked on polyester. The piece now hangs in a church in Fiji.

DIRECTIONS

The cross and the alleluia are both couched with silk sewing thread over #8 Japanese gold and outlined with gold twist. The leaves are worked in a long and short stitch in shades of green silk. The flowers are done in shades of red silk, with yellow centers and little green leaves around the edge. A satin stitch is used for all areas except the shaded part of the petals, which is done in long and short. The outer edge of each petal is padded with felt before it is covered with a satin stitch. All outlining and stems are worked in #8 Japanese gold and couched with silk sewing thread.

ALLELUIA

Little Fisherman

JUDITH SAVAGE BECKER

See Color Plate 28.

Photo by Don Servais.

Overall Size: 7½″ x 7½″.

This piece is a twentieth-century design using seventeenth-century stump work techniques but not materials.

MATERIALS

#14 blue Aida cloth, 14″ x 14″
Piece of linen twill or other strong, closely woven cloth, 12″ x 12″
Scraps of calico, denim, nylon stocking
Piece of string

Piece of corn husk, burlap, or similar material
Small stick or twig
  Floss: dark, medium, and light green; royal and light blue; orange; medium yellow; medium and light gold; light olive; kelly green; light and dark olive green; medium and light pink; tan; flesh tone; black; dark, medium, and light gray; red; white; and beige.
  Wool: dark, medium, and light gray; dark, medium, and light brown; beige; rust; brick red; black; off-white; dark and light straw; and dark, medium, and light tree brown.

DIRECTIONS

  Transfer design to the Aida cloth, leaving out the boy and dog. Transfer figures of the boy and dog to linen twill or other suitable material.
  Stitch and color instructions follow, for various parts of the design:

Grass

Cross-stitch, three shades green floss, starting at the top of grass line, darkest shade at top.

Cottage

Side of main building and side and front of secondary building: Continental stitch, medium gray wool
Front of main building: Slanted Gobelin, blend of medium gray and medium brown wool
Roof of main building: Interlocking Gobelin, blend of beige and gold wool (work stem stitch in gold wool around roof)
Roof of secondary building: Interlocking Gobelin, beige wool
Windows and door outlines: Outline stitch, dark brown wool
Door and shutters: Satin stitch, blend of medium brown and rust wool
Chimney: Brick stitch, brick red wool for front and dark brown wool for side

Trees

Smaller tree near house: Rows of split stitch, medium brown wool
Larger tree near house: Rows of chain stitch, three shades brown wool
Tree near boy: Rows of chain stitch, three shades tree brown wool

Bird and Nest

Bird's body: Split stitch, royal blue, light blue, and orange floss (filling in a highlight with light blue)
Bird's eye: French knot, black floss
Bird's beak: Straight stitches, orange floss
Bird's legs: Straight stitches, orange floss
Nest: Straight stitches, two shades straw-colored wool
Eggs: Satin stitch, light blue floss

Bridge
Stem stitch, dark brown wool

Rocks
Satin stitch, three shades gray floss

Lilies, Lily Pads, and Frog
Lilies: Satin stitch, medium and light pink floss
Pads: Buttonhole stitch, light olive green floss
Frog: Split stitch, kelly green floss
Frog's eye: French knot, white floss

Flowers by Stream
Petals: Lazy daisy stitch, yellow floss
Centers: French knots, light gold floss
Leaves: Split stitch, two shades olive green floss

Stream
Ripples in water: Stem stitch, light blue floss

Fishing Equipment
Worm can (outside): Satin stitch, tan floss
Worm can (inside): Satin stitch, black floss
Bobber (top): Satin stitch, white floss
Bobber (bottom): Satin stitch, red floss

With all shades of green floss, using random straight stitches, place threads to look like grass along the edges of the stream.

DIRECTIONS FOR CREATING DETACHED PIECES

Dog
Use split stitch in shades of brown, beige, and off-white wool to complete the dog. Top-stitch the dog's eyes and spots in white.

Boy
For the boy, select a bright print cotton fabric and cut it out to fit the shirt area. Cut the fabric with a ¼-inch seam allowance for turning under the raw edges. Stitch directly to the design, leaving the sleeves open at the wrist areas.

From a scrap of soft denim, cut fabric to the shape of the overalls, adding a ¼-inch seam allowance for turning under the raw edges; leave plenty of material for folding up the cuffs. Stitch directly to the design, easing in the denim to fit the shape.

For the boy's feet, use satin stitch in dark brown wool.

For his face, cut the face's shape from an index card, extending the shape under the boy's hairline. Place a small piece of polyester fiberfill on top of the card shape. Then draw a scrap of stocking over the fill and the card to the back; pull taut and secure by twisting and then sewing. Cut off the excess at the back. Add features to the face. Place the face in position and blind-stitch through from back to secure.

For the hands, complete these in the same way as for the face, molding them to fit the correct shapes. Tuck ends of material into the shirtsleeves and blind-stitch down. Leave room to put the fishing pole through the hands.

For the boy's hair, use straight stitches in warm brown wool. Create hair coming out at the part line and stitch to the outside.

For his hat, cut out of dried corn husk, burlap, or any suitable material the crown of the hat. With beige floss, blind-stitch to the backing. Cut the brim to fit the shape and blind-stitch in place.

DIRECTIONS FOR FINISHING DETACHED PIECES

Turn both figures to the back. Clip off excess threads. Using colorless fingernail polish, paint the entire area, extending over edges by at least ¼". Allow to dry completely. This secures all the edges and makes the figures rigid. Cut out both figures, cutting as closely as possible to the edges. Place figures in proper position and blind-stitch to the background, taking care that none of the tacking stitches show on the front.

Place a proper size stick through the hands of the little boy and secure by stitching the ends of the hands down over the stick and placing a few extra tack-down stitches over the stick where they will not be seen.

With perle cotton or thin string threaded on a sharp needle, bring the string up through the back of the bobber, unthread from the needle, and, pulling the thread fairly tight, tie the end to the end of the fishing pole with a bow knot.

Diamond

SHAY PENDRAY

Photo by Jack Kausch.

See Color Plate 29.

Overall Size: 6″ x 6″.

MATERIALS

 #18 royal uni canvas, 12″ x 12″
 Dark French silk, twenty-five strands, 40″ long
 Medium French silk, twenty-two strands, 40″ long
 Light French silk, ten strands, 40″ long
 One skein dark shade Marlitt
 Two skeins light shade Marlitt
 Six skeins Zwicky Swiss silk
 One card silver cloisonné

DIRECTIONS

 1. Find the center hole of the canvas.
 2. Draw miter lines out from the center hole, radiating out twenty-six meshes in all four directions.
 3. Count up thirty-two holes. *Count the center hole as hole number 1.* Bring the needle up in hole 32 and go down in hole 36. This is the peak stitch of the Florentine pattern.

4. The Florentine pattern is worked toward the center. The charted row is worked with Zwicky Swiss silk, 8–10 ply (light). The next six rows should be worked as follows: row 2, darkest shade French silk, 7 ply; row 3, lightest shade French silk, 7 ply; row 4, medium shade French silk, 7 ply; row 5, cloisonné; row 6, Zwicky Swiss silk (same as row 1); row 7, darkest shade French silk.

5. Once these rows are completed, count up seventeen threads from the top of uppermost Swiss silk peak Florentine stitch (marked with x) and mark the hole above the seventeenth thread (marked with a zero). Do this on all four sides.

6. Draw a diagonal line connecting all four holes (marked with A). This forms a diamond. Stitch this diamond with French silk of darkest shade, 7 ply, following the Florentine pattern.

7. Draw a straight line out from the zero-marked hole to form a square. Inside this square, stitch the Gobelin border. For the straight lines of the border, use lightest shade French silk, 7 ply. For the squiggle lines, use (1) Gobelin squiggle stitch with dark shade Marlitt, 8 ply, and (2) Smyrna cross-stitch with medium shade Marlitt, 4 ply.

For the leaf-stitch border, alternate (1) lightest shade French silk, 5 ply, (2) lightest shade Marlitt, 6 ply, and (3) lightest shade Swiss silk, 6 ply.

Behind the leaves, fill with basketweave French silk in darkest shade, 4 ply.

For the padded Scotch stitch border, use the darkest shade French silk, 5 ply. The center stitch of the Scotch stitch is done in cloisonné.

A detailed sketch with stitch and shading instructions for the upper left quarter of Diamond follows, on pages 144 and 145.

Diamond

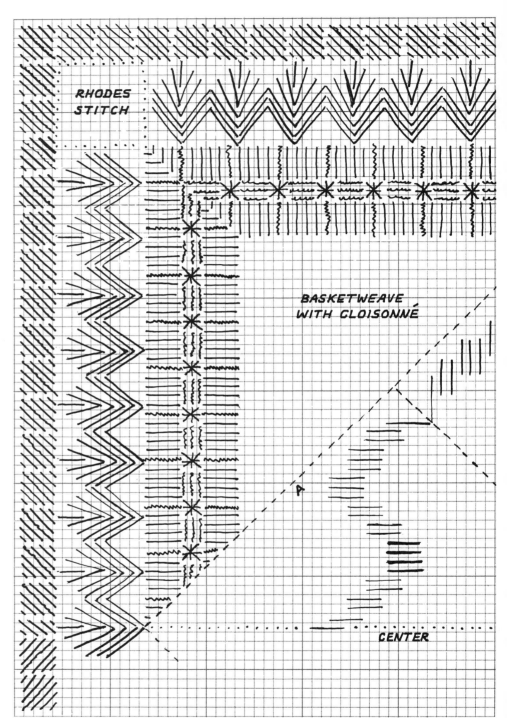

RHODES
STITCH

BASKETWEAVE
WITH CLOISONNÉ

CENTER

1. From the center to the bottom of the bargello
pattern there are thirty-two holes, counting
the center hole as number 1.

2. From the top of the bargello pattern to the
leaf stitch there are seventeen holes.

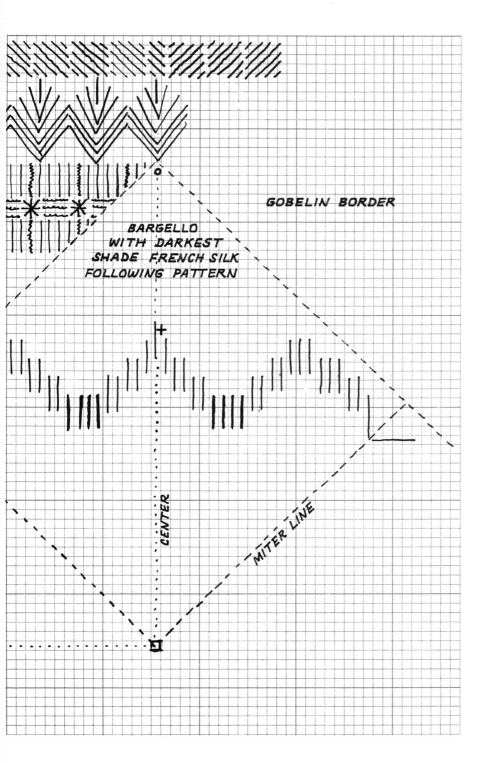

GOBELIN BORDER

BARGELLO
WITH DARKEST
SHADE FRENCH SILK
FOLLOWING PATTERN

CENTER

MITER LINE

Medallion

SHAY PENDRAY

See Color Plate 30.

Photo by Jack Kausch.

Overall Size: 6" x 6".

MATERIALS

    #18 royal uni canvas, 12" x 12"
    Two cards Elsa Williams silk, peacock blue
    Two shades French silk, three strands, 40" long, green
    One skein Zwicky Swiss silk, blue
    One skein Marlitt, blue
    Silver metallic thread
    Twenty-five strands French silk, 40" long (for background)

DIRECTIONS

    Find the center hole and draw lines out of it to the north, south, east, and west. Each line should be fifty-two holes long, counting the center hole as number one.

    The charted row is the outer row of bias Florentine. Each row after is worked toward the center. The outer row is in Elsa Williams silk, 4 ply; the second row toward the center is in French silk, 5 ply; the third row toward the center is in

Zwicky Swiss silk, 6 ply; the fourth row toward the center is in French silk, 5 ply; the fifth row toward the center is in Marlitt, 4 ply; the sixth row toward the center is in Elsa Williams silk, 4 ply; the seventh row toward the center is in French silk, 5 ply.

When the bias Florentine is completed, count up fifteen holes from the outer row of the Florentine. From the fifteenth hole draw a diagonal line up thirteen holes. Connect this hole and the thirteenth hole via a straight line toward the bias Florentine. This makes the area to be filled in with silver metallic in diagonal mosaic stitch. Note the C's on the graph. The graph shows one of four areas completed in this stitch.

Fill the rest of the area with Scotch stitch and Gobelin, as charted.

Remaining areas are filled with basketweave. Note the slant of the stitch to go with the design.

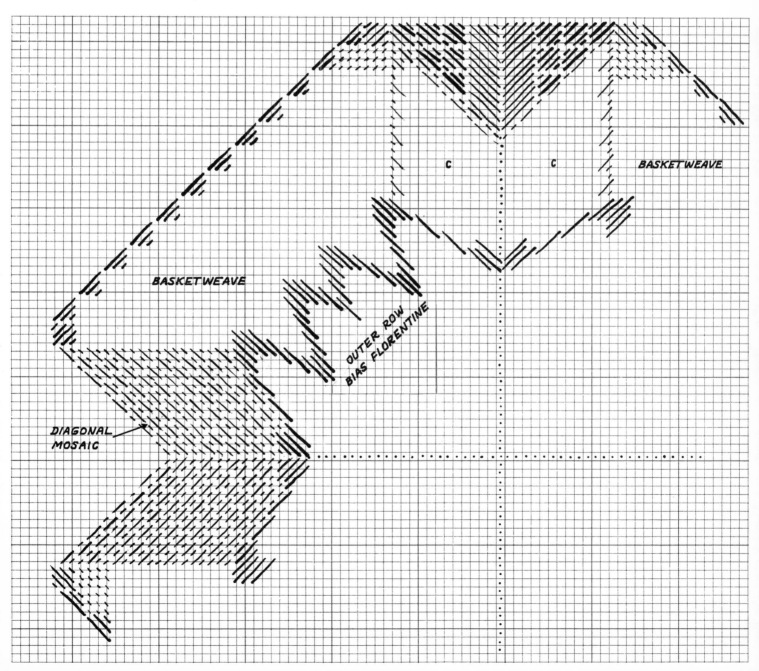

If God Be the Guide

GINNIE THOMPSON

Photo by McKenzie Dickerson.

See Color Plate 31.

Image Size: 202 x 147 threads.

Worked in counted cross-stitch on 28-count linen with one strand of Danish flower thread, the motto is from the embroideries done by Lady Holte, Aston Hall, Birmingham, England, in 1744. Although the words are English, the sampler is American in flavor. The muted colors and quilt pattern border are reminiscent of works of the Amish, Shakers, Quakers, Mennonites, or just plain vanilla American pioneers.

You will be working primarily with cross-stitch, but with some backstitch, too. Horizontal "C" and vertical "C," with arrows, point to your center starting place.

Color Key

■ Dull dark blue	o Light gray
+ Beige	Ǝ Gray
S Sand color	✗ Dark gray
✗ Earth color	◢ Darkest gray
● Deep dark brown	

BACKSTITCH DIRECTIONS

Mother
Mouth: Earth
Hands: Beige
Outline of face: Beige

Flowers
Stems: Beige

Little Boy with Mother
Eye: Dull dark blue
Mouth: Earth
Outline of face: Beige

Boy with Pig
Outline of face and hands: Beige
Pig detail: Earth color

Chicken
Detail: Earth

Girl
Outline of face and hands: Beige
Girl's bucket handle: Deep dark brown

Farmer
Mouth: Earth
Outline of hands: Beige

Cow
Cowbell chain: Light gray

Pitchfork
Dark Gray

Your initials may be worked in the border, if desired.

A design sketch for If God Be the Guide follows, on page 150.

ABCDEFGHIJK

LMNOPQRSTU

VWXYZ 1234567890

IF GOD BE THE GUIDE
THE WORK WILL ABIDE.

1977

Ginnie Thompson

Glory Be to God for Dappled Things

GINNIE THOMPSON

See Color Plate 32.

Image Size: 149 x 86 threads.

Worked in counted cross-stitch on 28-count linen with one strand of Danish flower thread, the thought is from a Gerard Manley Hopkins poem.

You will be working primarily with cross-stitch, but with some backstitch, too. Horizontal "C" and vertical "C," with arrows, point to your center starting place.

Color Key
X Dull brick red
▼ Red-brown
■ Dark red-brown
∟ Light carrot orange
∧ Dark carrot orange
O Orange-yellow
☐ Light fresh green
⁄⁄ Dark fresh green

A design sketch for Glory Be to God for Dappled Things follows, on page 152.